D0001686

Forgiveness

is ———————

POWER

A USER'S GUIDE TO WHY AND HOW TO FORGIVE

William Fergus Martin

PROPERTY OF
ALPINE PUBLIC LIBRARY
805 W. AVE E
ALPINE, TX 79830

 FINDHORN PRESS

© William Fergus Martin 2013

The right of William Fergus Martin to be identified as the
author of this work has been asserted by him in accordance
with the Copyright, Designs and Patents Act 1998.

Published in 2013 by Findhorn Press, Scotland

ISBN 978-1-84409-628-2

All rights reserved.

The contents of this book may not be reproduced in any form,
except for short extracts for quotation or review,
without the written permission of the publisher.

A CIP record for this title is available from the British Library.

Edited by Michael Hawkins
Cover design by Richard Crookes
Interior design by Damian Keenan
Printed and bound in the EU

Published by
Findhorn Press
117-121 High Street,
Forres IV36 1AB,
Scotland, UK

t +44 (0)1309 690582
f +44 (0)131 777 2711
e info@findhornpress.com
www.findhornpress.com

Contents

Contents

DEDICATION

To Tomoko, my lovely wife,
who expresses forgiveness
so consistently and so beautifully

Acknowledgements

Every book has at least three writers; the author, the editor and the hidden Muse who provides inspiration. My heartfelt thanks go to Michael Hawkins, as editor, for his wonderful efforts into helping craft this book into something that will help many people.

My thanks also to the tireless team at Findhorn Press, particularly Sabine Weeke and Carol Shaw, for seeing the need and the value of this work.

My final thanks go to the Muse who dropped so many good ideas into my head (about how forgiveness can be practical, usable and accessible) that I just had to release my resistance and write a book to get them out. Special mentions go to William Bloom, Dorothy Lippincott and Lynn Barton for their very helpful comments early on and to Caroline Myss whose workshop on the Seven Graces helped inspire the Entitlement section.

William Fergus Martin

Introduction

Are you as forgiving as you would like to be? If not, then this book is for you as it makes forgiveness practical, usable and accessible.

We all want the freedom, peace of mind and happiness, which forgiveness brings. It is one thing to want to forgive; it is another to really be able to do it. This book shows you how by giving you *four simple steps* you can use to practice forgiveness. You also get many additional ideas and exercises to broaden your understanding and improve your forgiveness skills.

This is a practical book on Forgiveness: it's a User Guide on how to forgive. Virtually every chapter has exercises which you can use to experience the points made within that chapter. This helps you learn how to forgive and free yourself from the past, so that you can create your life anew.

This book makes no attempt to preach or try to convince you that you "should" forgive. Instead it lets you see and experience the benefits of forgiving. As you experience the lightness, well-being and sense of empowerment forgiveness brings you will naturally want more.

You don't need to be of any particular religion or philosophical persuasion to benefit from *Forgiveness is Power*. Whatever your current religious beliefs you will discover that becoming more skilled at forgiving will allow you to live more truly aligned with those beliefs.

The topics of some chapters may surprise you. Many of the chapters are intended to help create the type of attitudes, the kind of inner climate, where forgiveness can flourish. Therefore much of the material is about becoming reconciled with ourselves, and comfortable in our own skin, so that we are more able to feel forgiving.

It may seem unusual to think of Forgiveness as Power and to see it is a tool for self-empowerment. However, as you explore these pages, and particularly as you use the Four Steps to Forgiveness, you will find that there is no other way to adequately describe something that can so radically and dramatically change our lives for the better.

PART ONE

Forgiveness Is The Power to Choose

Why Forgive?

Forgiveness is the power to choose how things affect us.

In this chapter we look at the benefits we get from being more forgiving. This will help us to be motivated to forgive more readily as we will see the practical and useful things we can get out of it. We are then less likely to get distracted from developing forgiveness if life gets busy, or the situation is challenging.

When you forgive you win.

One good reason to forgive is that it means that you win. No matter what happened, forgive and you have won. You win, because you stop playing the loser. You will certainly feel much more like a winner when you forgive than if you don't. Once you have experienced the feeling of winning, which comes from forgiving, you will want to forgive anyone and everyone.

This is not the kind of winning which requires that someone else lose. What others do is up to them. Forgiveness offers you the chance to experience winning in every situation. It is not likely that you will feel bad about something when you come out of it feeling like a winner.

When you forgive you stop being a victim.

When you hold on to grudges and resentments then there is usually a feeling of being a victim as part of the package. Letting go of those grudges and resentments means letting go of the victim feeling also. If you do not feel like a victim then you do not behave like a victim, and you will not be a victim.

When you forgive you are free.

When you forgive you unhook yourself from the situation and from the others involved. If you really forgive you free yourself from all negative effects of whatever happened. You let go of any associated pain, shame, anger or guilt. If you feel stuck in a relationship, and you forgive the other person, you will find that you now feel much freer to either make it work, or to walk away. You are no longer bound to them and may wonder why on earth you got so caught up with them in the first place.

Forgiving lets you off the hook, not them.

Forgiveness lets you off the hook as it releases you from any sense of guilt or blame. It frees you from blaming yourself, and from the feeling that you should or could have done something differently.

Forgiveness does not let the other person off the hook. If they harmed you they are still responsible for having caused that pain or harm and will need to find their own way to resolving that. They may be facing the consequences already through ill health, misfortune, guilt, shame and remorse. Most people are good at punishing themselves even when they do not show it. You do not have to take on the job of teaching people their lessons. It is up to the process of evolution to do that, and you are unlikely to have the skills or wisdom to be up to that task (especially with someone you are angry at).

Forgiveness brings you more money.

Forgiveness can bring you more money when you stop letting old resentments get in the way of your abundance. If you hold a mean-spirited attitude to people who are better off than you then you will repel such people and they will not be able to help you. If you are envious of them you will not be able to comfortably associate with them and learn from them.

Letting go of ill feelings towards those who have more money than you allows you to become like them as otherwise your unconscious thoughts will stop you becoming like someone you judge as bad or unlikeable.

Forgiveness improves your sex life.

Forgiveness helps you feel more free, open and able to create better relationships. It makes it easier for you to have empathy and understanding towards others and their needs. This makes you more attractive to other people on every level. It also makes you a more attentive, and interesting lover as you will be much more present.

Forgiveness reduces bad feelings.

Think of someone you have not forgiven and notice the effect this has on your body. Notice what it does to your breathing, your heartbeat and how it feels in your belly. Chances are the experience of unforgiveness will be uncomfortable, heavy and possibly painful. You will probably feel depleted and lack energy afterwards.

In this way we can plainly see that unforgiveness is not a neutral state but a very active state that uses up our energy. It uses energy we could be using in more happy and productive ways. We may block out our awareness of the feelings so as to be able to carry on with life, but they will still be there. By developing the habit of forgiveness we free ourselves from many heavy, depressing and debilitating experiences. We then have more energy for happy, productive and enjoyable experiences.

Forgiveness reduces fear and brings peace of mind.

As you learn the art of Forgiveness you will have less fear, stress and anxiety. You know that if you make mistakes you can handle the consequences. You are less concerned about what will happen in life because you know that you have the right attitude to turn things to your greater good.

Forgiveness makes your life safer.

As you become more forgiving you become more conscious and more aware. You are more able to hold a detached perspective and less likely to be pulled into someone else's unhappy game, or be caught out by their dubious intentions. You become less reactive and less likely to create unhappiness for yourself, or others. You are less motivated by guilt, greed and fear and therefore much less prone to being manipulated into doing things against your own best interest.

Forgiveness makes you wiser.

You gain more from your experiences if you have a well-developed capacity to forgive (see chapter *Be wounded, or Be Wise*). If you feel bitter, cynical or are wracked in pain about an event, you are not likely to have gained anything much other than fear and aversion. Your mind will be too clouded to see possible benefits you can gain, or insights you can learn from it.

Forgiveness makes whatever you can gain from an experience more accessible. It clears your mind and allows you to see anything that is good, redeeming, or constructive about the situation.

Forgiveness lets in life's goodness.

If you look at someone you know who is bitter and resentful you can see how this locks them inside themselves. It makes them unavailable to much of the goodness or kindness which could come their way. Their grumpiness and bitterness keeps at bay those who could and would help them.

Any form of unforgiveness has the same effect. Your unforgiveness, even if seemingly mild, also to some extent blocks goodness and kindness, which could flow towards you.

Forgiveness connects you with life.

The more you have not forgiven the more you feel numb, lonely, isolated and disconnected from the flow of life. Forgiveness reconnects you with life and with other people. It frees you from the self-made prison you create if you put a fearful or angry shell around yourself as a misguided form of protection. It allows you access to the experiences of beauty, wonder and delight which make life worthwhile, and which an unforgiving mind cannot see or experience.

Forgiveness frees you from pain.

Through forgiveness you experience less hurt, less guilt, less shame, less disappointment, less bitterness, and less resentment. You experience less of these things because you no longer encourage the kind of thinking which supports those feelings.

When you forgive you succeed.

Whatever your idea of success, you find that when you successfully forgive you experience a surprisingly intense sense of triumph. When you forgive you have indeed triumphed. You have succeeded in doing your part in prevailing over the darkness and ignorance, which is the cause of so much human suffering. This is the ultimate in success: success in living from the best that is within you.

You will also be more available to successful people as they will see your open, positive attitude and respond accordingly. You will attract the types of ideas and the types of people who will help you succeed in whatever direction you choose.

Forgiveness makes you confident.

If you lack confidence it is because you do not feel that you know how to handle a particular situation. When you cultivate a forgiving attitude you can go in to new situations with a strong sense of knowing what to do. Whatever happens you will develop your forgiveness skills and you will extract life-enhancing benefits from it. You are confident that you have a strategy for every event and situation: to be forgiving.

Forgiveness empowers you.

Forgiveness is the power to choose how things affect you. You are no longer simply at the mercy of fate. Whatever your circumstances, whatever has befallen you, it enables you to rise above. You can at least neutralize, and very often benefit from, situations which otherwise would have left you wounded or debilitated.

Forgiveness brings you more love.

In confronting the areas of your life where you have been holding an unforgiving attitude you unlock your potential for greater connection with others, deeper compassion for those who lash out blindly and wider comprehension of the causes of events. You begin to dismantle your unloving patterns of thinking and behaviour. The more you learn to forgive the more you are able to access your capacity to love.

Forgiveness gives you a renewed sense of meaning and purpose.

As you learn to forgive a new sense of purpose grows within you. Even apparently meaningless, daunting or downright negative experiences can be turned around. They all become part of how you learned to forgive. This gives even the greyest or darkest of experiences a profound meaning and deep purpose.

Forgiveness can save a relationship.

Forgiveness can save a marriage, reunite estranged families, heal embittered relationships. It can also free you from unhealthy entanglements to create better connections with others.

Forgiveness brings you better health.

Many studies show that developing a forgiving attitude increases health and well-being in deep and profound ways. It is not hard to see why this would be the case. Through the practice of forgiveness we stop having the kind of thinking which stresses our nervous system.

Although many studies link forgiveness to psychological health, studies which link forgiveness to specific *physical* health benefits are rare. However the relationship between stress and physical health is well documented and with forgiveness having such a profound effect on reducing stress levels it is reasonable to assume that it also brings definite benefits to physical health too.

EXERCISES

We will revisit some of the points in this section in depth later. For now try the exercises below to strengthen your own willingness to forgive.

- Make a list, in your own words, of the ways in which you gain by forgiving: have another look at the above if you need some reminders.
- Read your list to yourself (out loud if possible) every morning and evening for a week or for a month.

What is Forgiveness?

Forgiveness is choosing to be happy.

Our assumptions about forgiveness, and what it is, may not be true. Having a clear idea as to what forgiveness is, and what it is not, is a good beginning to enabling ourselves to forgive more effectively. There are many definitions of forgiveness and we will explore more of them later, but let us use a simple and basic one to start with. Forgiveness is letting go of the desire to punish.

Forgiveness can be as much about letting go of the desire to punish ourselves as it is about letting go of the desire to punish other people. Forgiveness is not the same thing as reconciliation (more about reconciliation later), which is where we choose to re-establish a relationship with someone. Forgiveness is simply freeing ourselves from wanting to punish. This is a significant freedom that leads to many other freedoms.

For a few minutes, stop and think about someone you want to punish. Notice how it feels in your body to want vengeance or want to punish this person. When you notice all the stress and bad feelings that this creates in your body, you may wonder if it isn't you who is being punished instead! An unforgiving state of mind is not neutral. An unforgiving mind at best feels numb and at worst feels highly negative and caustic. This is obviously not a happy state to be in.

Being unforgiving has high opportunity costs.

We pay a high price in lost happiness for not being forgiving. In business they talk about Opportunity Cost. Opportunity Cost is the cost of investing in one thing instead of another. Wanting to punish has a huge Opportunity Cost. Every moment we are in that state, we lose opportunities to be happy, to be creative, and to enjoy life and the people around us.

A strongly unforgiving state can send us into spells of being miserable and complaining, angry and spiky, or of being sullen and uncommunicative. Hardly anyone may be able to reach us at those times. Even if we do not say a word about it to anyone we pay the Opportunity Cost for holding on to wanting to punish. Our tone of voice, our facial expression, how we walk and how we stand are all subtly or blatantly affected – all for the worse.

We are also diverted from being in the present moment as part of our attention is lurking in an unhappy event and in holding desperately to the intention of making sure it does not happen again. Yet that very attitude blinds us in ways which makes it more likely to happen again.

If we look at our desire to punish, and all the things we have to do to maintain and fulfil that desire, we can see how lack of forgiveness wrecks our chances of being happy and having peace of mind. As soon as we hold the thought of wanting to punish someone we immediately start to hurt ourselves from the stresses this creates. When we hold onto thoughts of wanting to make someone else unhappy we are losing chances to be truly happy ourselves. We could even say that Forgiveness is choosing to be happy.

We experience what we intend for others

When I was in my early teens at school there was a group of "toughs" who hung around together. I found myself wondering whether I wanted to be one of them. I watched them from a distance a few times and soon realized that they seemed unhappy somehow. When they weren't giving someone outside of their group a hard time they were busy giving each other a hard time. I decided that I would rather be happy than be like them and that being a "tough guy" was not for me.

Of course such "tough guy" posturing can be an attempt to hide insecurity. As movies and TV programmes often highlight (whether intentionally or not), people whose lives are based on violence or aggression live in constant fear of violence and aggression themselves. Such extreme cases demonstrate most clearly that the way we think about others is the way we assume others think about us. A genuine, open, easy and happy smile does not sit well on the face of a "tough guy" – at least not for very long. While we are not as extreme as that (hopefully) this does help to illustrate that we live on the same level of experience that we want to create for others.

While we are in an unforgiving state of mind, and holding a variety of angry, bitter and spiteful thoughts, we are the ones who are suffering. Such thoughts and feelings are an intense form of unhappiness. Can we feel hate and be happy? Can we feel bitter and be happy? Can we feel vengeful and be truly happy? No we cannot. There is a sick sense of satisfaction from vengeance, but that is not genuine happiness. Unforgiveness and happiness just do not go together. Forgiveness is partly a process of letting go of our own suffering.

Why do we want to do harm?

If we feel that we have been harmed we may feel justified in doing harm in return. Why? Where does that come from? Does it feel like a response that is healthy and life enhancing? If we feel into that state as it arises in our body we will notice all the warning signs of something bad happening inside us. Granted that part of our reaction will be around what we feel the other person did to us, but much of it is what we want to do to them. Our body will exhibit fairly obvious increased levels of stress and anxiety when we want to harm someone.

What we do in defence usually seems like an attack to the other person. Our attempt to counter-attack may feel like an unjustified attack to them. This simply escalates the situation. Unless there is some kind of truce, it either goes into a continuous loop till nobody can remember who really started it, or eventually someone "wins" and someone "loses".

Most movies use a particular formula to get us to want to see the baddie get hurt. Early in the movie they show the baddie doing something mean, wicked or horrible. This sets us against the baddie so that whenever the goodie comes along and gives that baddie his just comeuppance it all seems right and proper to us.

This formula is used in movies of almost every kind from old-fashioned to modern high-tech ones filled with computer-generated special effects. Movies make a point of getting us to dislike the baddie so we do not object to them getting hurt. You may notice that in some movies the difference between the goodie and the baddie is not in their behaviour but in the "justification" they have for their actions. The goodie may do as many harmful things as the baddie, but as they are the good guy the movie plot makes it seem right by how the sequence of events is shown. If we saw the good guy hurting the bad guy first we would think they are the bad guy.

Isn't this trick the movies play not also a trick we play on ourselves? When we want vengeance it is easier to focus on what we think is bad about the other person rather than to think anything good about them. We play the same trick with each other too. If we want our friends to take our side against someone we tell them all we can think of that is bad about the other person. We may even exaggerate here and there to make the point. We may tell ourselves that they are the baddie after all, so we can do that to them as we are the goodie (or at least the innocent victim).

The more unforgiving we are the more likely we are to step into being the baddie. We may dress up our attacks as counter-attacks and say that we are only defending ourselves, but that does not make them any the less of an attack to the recipient. This perpetuates the cycle of attack and counter-attack. It is quite possible for there to be two baddies with each of them protesting that they are the goodie. One of those baddies may be us.

If we want to know what role we are playing in a situation we need to look at our present feelings and motives. Are we motivated by kindness and compassion or fear and anger? Is it our intention to help or to hurt? If we are out to do damage, and feel justified in doing so, then we need to question our motives and actions very carefully.

Anger is useful when it helps us take a stance against an injustice, but we have to be careful if we think that gives us the right to inflict pain on others. Anger as a motive needs something to ennoble it (such as compassion for those we think are the cause of a situation) if we are to be less likely to drift into harmful behaviour. Otherwise our attempt to redress one injustice will cause us to create other injustices.

Justice

Forgiveness does not stop us seeking justice, as justice is not the same thing as vengeance. Justice is also not necessarily the same thing as the desire to punish. Justice usually includes restricting the ways in which someone can cause further harm. If we are harmed by someone who is a hardened criminal, or if they show no sign of remorse, then it is better for wider society to be protected from that person – at least for a while. We can forgive someone and still choose to support the process whereby they go to prison. If we have access to Restorative Justice then that could be a highly effective way of achieving both forgiveness and justice.

In forgiveness we can include justice, but we do so without an intention to cause harm. We let go of needing to cast someone else as bad. In forgiveness we begin to let go of playing these kinds of tricks on ourselves and let go of playing them on others too.

If we look more closely we see that our defensiveness is often what harms us the most. Our ways of defending ourselves often causes us more pain than the original hurt. The original hurt may have lasted only a very short time, but by hanging on to the pain, and not forgiving, we extend it to last a long time. Our fear that the hurt may happen again, or our unwillingness to let go, makes us hang on to old pain. If we hold onto wanting to punish we pay the price in terms of immediate loss of well-being and lost opportunity. If we hold onto wanting to punish we end up punishing ourselves with all the bad feelings that we experience. Forgiveness helps us to let go and set ourselves free.

Try this:

1. Next time you are watching a movie notice how you feel about the baddie. Notice how the plot will awaken a dislike for the baddie and how you feel when the baddie "gets what he deserves". Do you ever cast someone as the baddie in a story by describing only their bad points (possibly exaggerated) to another person?

2. Is there someone in your life who has hurt you and you want to retaliate against them? Is it possible that they would see your counter-attack as an unjustified attack?

Reconciliation

Fear is wisdom as a child.

Forgiveness and reconciliation are two distinct and different things. It is important to understand this otherwise our fear or dislike of someone can cause us to hold back from forgiving them. Whereas, forgiveness is letting go of the desire to punish; reconciliation is the re-establishing of a relationship. Forgiveness and reconciliation often go together and this causes some confusion between them. However, there are some very important differences between forgiveness and reconciliation.

Forgiveness is always possible, but reconciliation is not always possible. We may not be able to reconcile with someone because they may have died, or because we have no way to contact them, but we can always forgive them. This shows that we do not need to be reconciled with someone in order to forgive them. In other words, the choice to forgive someone is different from the choice to reconcile with them. Deciding not to reconcile may even make it easier to forgive, as we may be holding back out of fear that they will harm us again.

Reconciliation may not be desirable if the other person is very likely to re-offend. They may be a career criminal, a persistent abuser, or someone who denies even to themselves that they did anything wrong, or that we were hurt. If they maintain an aggressive stance against us, "What's your problem!" then reconciliation is much more problematic though it is still possible to forgive. Even though we forgive someone we still have the right to protect ourselves from the other's behaviour. Forgiveness does not mean that we choose to be a doormat.

Putting up with someone is not the same as forgiving them. We may put up with someone's behaviour because we fear that we will be worse off without them. When we truly forgive someone we do not put up with bad behaviour, at least not for long. We are then free to make wiser choices not based on fear. This means that we may forgive someone and still walk away from a relationship with them. Becoming reconciled is also about becoming reconciled with ourselves and our own deepest needs and our own highest aspirations. If being with someone makes it impossible to be reconciled with ourselves then we could choose to forgive them, but not be reconciled with them.

Forgiveness is unconditional, but reconciliation is not. Forgiveness does not require us to stay with the person. We may need some distance before we can even start the process of forgiving. It is hard to forgive someone while they are still hurting us. It is possible, but it is harder. Forgiveness is not dependent on us having any contact with the other person at all. Reconciliation with them obviously requires us to be in contact, but forgiveness is independent of any contact.

If we assume that forgiveness has to include reconciliation then this can block us from forgiving. This is especially true if it is someone likely to hurt us again. In some circumstances we have the right to expect to see evidence of their true remorse before we are reconciled with them. We need to be careful with this one, as it may be vengeance in disguise and "wanting to see them crawl". However, it is also true that without true remorse it is possible they will do the same thing again. Some people seem to get caught in an offending/guilt loop. They offend, they feel guilty, they offend again, they feel guilty, and so on. It is as if their need to feel guilty, or to prove that they are guilty, drives their behaviour. Such a person is not someone we can reconcile with unless there are very strong limits on their behaviour.

Sometimes reconciliation and forgiveness are a step-by-step process where we forgive a little, reconcile a little, forgive some more, and so on. There are often such stories in the news media such as when an errant husband is gradually brought back into the bosom of his family. The husband may need to prove his fidelity to his wife over a period of time before he is fully reconciled with her and before he is fully forgiven.

We need to balance protecting ourselves with the fact that an act of forgiveness, possibly including some form of reconciliation, may be the very thing that transforms the person's life. Forgiveness can be a powerful form of transformation for us and for the other person. This is especially true if it takes the form of Restorative Justice, or the like, which has been shown to greatly reduce repeat offences. It also reduces the level of the offence by those who do re-offend, as they do things that are less harmful. However, Restorative Justice offers inbuilt forms of protection and that is why it works so well as it reduces the fear of being further harmed.

Fear often gets in the way of both forgiveness and reconciliation. Looking for ways to protect ourselves from further harm can greatly assist us in forgiving, and in becoming reconciled if we choose that too. Why should we set ourselves up to be harmed again? Folly is not forgiveness.

•••••

A while back I took some sound equipment needing repair to a hi-fi shop owned by a guy whom I vaguely knew. I contacted him later to see how the repair was going and after him giving me many excuses for many weeks I realized that he had probably lost my equipment (or sold it to someone – who knows). I went to his shop to try and resolve the matter, and was treated to a bizarre pantomime. He brought something from his storeroom and proclaimed, "Here it is!" Yet, it was not even vaguely like what I had left with him – and it obviously belonged to some other hapless customer. When I told him that was not "it" he got on the phone to "the manufacturer", made a show of speaking to them disparagingly and obnoxiously for a few minutes, and after hanging up, rolled his eyes dramatically, sighed and said, "See what I have to deal with?"

I left saying I would give him more time to find my equipment. After a while of hearing nothing I finally wrote a letter threatening to sue him and began to explore the options. Yet I had my doubts about the wisdom of this as I had also come away with a feeling that this guy was borderline... *something*.... It looked to me like there was something wrong with the wiring of the sound system of his mind.

I began to realize that I would need to hold myself in a state of being angry, tense and frustrated for months in order to take legal action against him. I asked around and found out this guy tended to leave a trail of trouble with his customers. It was like he was using the legal system to play out a need to be punished. After some deliberation (and a long walk along a deserted beach stamping and swearing), I decided to let it go, but to do so in a way that worked for me. I sent him a letter saying I was not intending to sue him after all and that I was going to let the matter drop. I told him it was up to him if he wanted put things straight by sending me replacement equipment or a refund, but that was the end of it as far as I was concerned.

It could be argued that he got away with it. Yes, that is true. He did get away with it. The point is that I let him get away with it, rather than choosing to attack him. I made sure that I did this in a way which I would be at peace with and would not feel ashamed about later. Sending an honest letter seemed at the time like the middle ground between doing nothing and suing him.

Another choice would have been to sue him and justify this by hoping that it would stop him doing the same to others. Yet, it looked to me like it would not have worked out that way. From what I could see there was something not quite right about his mental health. With this particular person, in that particular situation, and due to my own life circumstances at that time, I made the choice to let it go. In other situations I might choose differently.

Did this story have a happy ending – yes! I got back my peace of mind. I felt very relieved that the whole thing was over, as far as I was concerned. I did not get the equipment back, but I got my life back. He made no attempt at restitution and he expressed no remorse, so I never went back to that shop. I won back my sense of well-being. Whether he won or lost anything had nothing to do with me.

Situations can be messy and there is often no one right answer. It is often impossible (and it can just get in the way) to try to figure out other peoples' motives. All we can do is live by the highest principles we can manage in that situation and let life take its course. Treating people in a forgiving way, but not becoming a doormat, is a skill and all skills take practise. Practise means getting it wrong sometimes. It also means sometimes not even knowing whether we got it right or wrong. The main thing is to just do our best and move on.

Bridge Building

Sometimes it can be hard to show remorse. It can be difficult to take the initiative and offer a straight upfront apology. There may be feelings of shame and this seems to be one of the harder emotions for most of us to deal with. We may be hoping that they did not notice our misdemeanour, or they might be hoping that we were not really hurt or offended.

If it is an important relationship, it can be well worth making it easier for a person we need to forgive to reconnect with us in a neutral situation. This gives them a chance to show their remorse indirectly to begin with. People sometimes show remorse by being particularly helpful and considerate and by going out of their way. This can be a way to make amends in a roundabout way rather than specifically addressing what might be a delicate issue.

This kind of behaviour can be part of the dance of reconciliation. It may be a way of leading up to an apology: an apology that might never happen if snubbed in its early stages. It is important to look out for those early signs of bridge building and of making amends and give the person a chance, so that they can get past their shame enough to get to an open apology.

In the story above, it may be that if I had gone into the guy's shop and chatted to him as if nothing had happened, he may have relented and shown signs of wishing to make amends. He might have shown remorse indirectly by being particularly helpful, offering me a very good deal on a piece of equipment and so on. I have used this approach before to give someone a chance to make amends indirectly. Sometimes it works and sometimes it doesn't. I had a feeling that in this case it would not help so I let it go.

Angry Joe

Sometimes a situation will be right in our face and we need to sort out the forgiveness and reconciliation quickly. One day I found a very angry and indignant email in my inbox, which had gone to my boss and all the other managers at my work. It was from Joe who was one of the Computer Support staff whom I managed. Joe was a fiery character and in his email he was complaining bluntly and bitterly about a mistake he felt I had made and he went on to say that anyone who could do such a thing was not suitable to be a manager. Not a pleasant thing to read especially knowing that my boss and co-managers were reading it too! I went for a long walk at lunchtime to let off steam, then arranged a private meeting between Joe and myself.

At the meeting with Joe I pointed out that when any of the other managers asked about the Computer Team I always spoke constructively and said what a good team we had and how well everyone worked together. I also mentioned that I had defended him recently and spoke up for him when one of the other managers had asked whether Joe had been the cause of a problem in of one the departments. I asked him to bear that in mind and said, "Can you understand why I was not happy seeing someone who I have defended broadcast a mistake I had made to all the managers, including my boss, instead of talking to me about it beforehand?"

At first he defended his action, but eventually said he got the point and said he could understand how I felt. He understood it even better when I added that managers are more likely to react against someone who attacks another manager, and close ranks against the attacker, as they worry that the attacker is going to have a go at them next. I pointed out that I may well have to defend him because of his email about me, but I would do so.

After more of this sort of discussion Joe was beginning to look a bit horrified about sending that email, so I told him not to worry about it and that I would patch things up with the other managers if needed. I got on fairly well with Joe after that so there was some reconciliation, but I was not completely sure that he had really changed. I thought maybe he had just got better at keeping himself in check.

An interesting thing about the story of Joe is that it was possible to have some reconciliation simply because his behaviour changed – at least towards me. I left that job after some months and later heard that Joe got into trouble for becoming belligerent and swearing at colleagues and clients. His underlying attitude had not really changed, but it had still been possible for me to create a working relationship with him.

• • • • •

However, such reconciliations may depend on the communications skills we can muster at the time. I did not challenge Joe directly and say that I thought what he did was wrong. I just asked if he could understand how I felt about it. I did not actually ask him to change or to do anything differently. I just kept firmly coming back to saying, "This is how I feel, can you understand that?" This is what turned the situation around, rather than it blowing up into something worse. Possibly, when he got to the point of saying "Yes" and acknowledged how I felt, this awakened a sense of empathy in him towards me and made it harder for him to cast me in the role of "them". I was speaking to him the whole time as someone whom I saw as being in the same team as me. I was looking for mutual understanding and mutual respect, not to blame or punish.

Again I was looking for some kind of middle ground. I did not back away from facing Joe on my own, but neither did I try to attack him. I did not overtly try to make him wrong, but I did let him know what I felt was right. We both knew that I was his boss, but I did not rub that in his face and used my position to negotiate for something to both our benefit. I did get his agreement that in future he would bring any such complaints to me first, so I felt that reconciled with him enough to be able to maintain our working relationship.

About a year later after I left that job, I bumped into Joe socially. He gave me a warm hello and surprised me with a big hug (that was not exactly his style), so maybe he got something from our interaction after all.

Try this:

1. Have you tended to assume that if you forgive someone you need to reconcile with them too? Does thinking of forgiveness and reconciliation as being different things help you to forgive?

2. Is there anyone who you would like to forgive, but definitely do not want a reconciliation with? Does fully accepting that you do not want reconciliation with them make it easier for you to forgive?

Tough Forgiveness

Forgiveness gives us the freedom to stay
and the freedom to walk away.

Just as the idea of Tough Love has helped clarify a healthy expression of love, the concept of Tough Forgiveness can help clarify a healthy expression of forgiveness especially when it comes to reconciliation. We apply Tough Forgiveness when we are open to a reconciliation, but want clear agreements about specific issues so that we are willing to go ahead. We may want to limit the types of contact we have with the other person. We may also want to specify the types of behaviour that we do not find acceptable and which will cause us to end or pause the reconciliation process. We may want agreement to do something to increase mutual understanding such as going to a counsellor together.

We want to forgive as that frees us and brings peace of mind. The act of forgiving also tends to cause our hearts to open, and we may find ourselves with a growing willingness to have a reconciliation. Yet, we also need to notice any warning signs so that we can choose the right path to reconciliation.

There is always the chance that our act of forgiveness may cause the other person to have an awakening and feel genuine remorse and the desire to make amends. However, the co-dependency movement has shown that when we put up with bad behaviour we are usually part of the problem. There is nothing transformative, freeing or life enhancing about "putting up" with harmful behaviour; whereas forgiveness is freeing and life enhancing.

In a co-dependent situation, where two people's patterns of addiction hook into each other, there is very little forgiveness present. The alcoholic, workaholic, or drug addict and their co-dependent partner tend to have reconciliations without any real forgiveness taking place. The ennobling qualities of forgiveness are not present if we are compromising our genuine needs out of fear of loss, such as when we stay in an abusive relationship because we are afraid that otherwise we will have no one.

Tough forgiveness means ensuring that the other person knows and respects how we feel – especially about the things they do which we feel pained by. If this kind of mutual respect is not present then there is no real relationship and no real grounds for reconciliation.

People caught up in a Guilt/Abuse loop can easily go from "I'm sorry, I'm sorry…" then back to being abusive very quickly, so their apology is not a sign that they have changed in any real way. Their apology is just a sign that they are feeling guilty, or afraid, and are temporarily willing to alter their behaviour – but that may not last long. Their guilt feelings are really all about them and what will happen to them if we retaliate.

A clearer sign of genuine change is if they show a capacity to empathize with how we feel; they may say something like, "You must have felt awful when I did that." This is a sign that something deeper is going on. It is not all just about them, they are connecting with our feelings – or at least trying to. That is a sign that a reconciliation may be possible.

• • • • •

As part of Tough Forgiveness we may want to make sure that they really understand how we felt about whatever they did. If they are avoiding connecting with our honest feelings then it is not likely that they are really willing to change their behaviour.

Reconciliation is not just a decision; it is a process. It is a process that may take time and may involve expressing a lot of honest feelings to the other person about how we felt. If we neglect that step we may have hidden resentment or feel like we sold ourselves short. We don't really serve anyone by minimizing how we felt in reaction to something they did. It is not that we are necessarily holding them responsible for our feelings, it is that we are asking them to respect those feelings.

Other people are not responsible for our depth of feeling. We could have a whole long history involved in an issue and the other person was just the trigger for a lot of deep feelings. Yet it is still important that our true feelings are out in the open and respected if we are going to create a reconciliation.

Tough Forgiveness does not mean we get to put the blame for everything we are unhappy about onto someone else. Sharing our feelings is not the same as blaming someone else for them. There is a world of difference between, "This is how I feel… and it is your fault," and simply saying, "This is how I feel…." The first is loaded with blame and judgement. The second is more of a mutually respectful expression of honest feelings.

If someone were to say to us, "You are in the relationship you deserve," and that does not make us feel good then that is a sign that we are in the wrong relationship. There is nothing noble about us sacrificing the life we really want for the sake of someone who actually has no real life, but only a set of compulsions and addictions. If we give in to manipulative behaviour through fear of confrontation, from feeling unworthy, or from being unable to set healthy boundaries (by not being able to say "no") then we are very likely setting ourselves up for more painful experiences. We are basically telling ourselves that what we want does not matter and that our feelings are not important.

We may decide that reconciliation is just not possible. Jean tries to avoid her mother as much as she can. She finds her mother's aggressively critical and judgmental attitude toward her hard to bear. Jean comments, "People say to me that I should tell my mother that I love her and then all will be well. Those who say that do not know my mother. She would just think I am weak and utterly despise me if I said that."

Jean is a sensible and well-adjusted person so she probably knows what she is talking about and is showing wisdom in keeping herself out of harm's way. If there is a serious breakdown in an important relationship, then our challenge is to become reconciled within ourselves about breaking off the relationship, or minimizing contact. We may need to keep a distance with the occasional check-in from time to time to see if there has been any change. People have the right to stay stuck and we have the right to not stick with them. Sometimes people with important roles in our lives are not willing to play out their role – at least not in the ways which we need or expect.

It is better to find other ways to have our needs met rather than waiting for such people to change. If they are not intending to change we can be sure that they won't.

If we are not ready to forgive someone, or not ready to reconcile with them, then we need to forgive ourselves and accept how we feel. In this way we can at least be reconciled with ourselves. We may need time to recover, to renew ourselves, and to restore our faith in life. Once we have more practice with both forgiving and reconciliation we will be more able to forgive, and perhaps even reconcile, with the more challenging ones.

Try this:

1. Are you able to tell someone how you feel without blaming them for your feelings?

2. Are there clear boundaries you could set with someone which (if they respected those boundaries) would make it easier to forgive them?

Four Steps To Forgiveness

Having specific processes or methods helps make it easier for us to forgive. The Four Steps to Forgiveness Worksheet that follows is a way to construct a Forgiveness Declaration. A Forgiveness Declaration helps us focus on forgiving a specific person, or a specific situation.

It is best to use the worksheet exactly as it is at least once. Later you can modify the method, or discover your own method. Once you get a sense of how it works, please feel free to make any changes that appeal to your instincts or intuition. Making changes, as your needs change, will help to keep your forgiveness work fresh. You will be more likely to stick with it by keeping it interesting rather than letting it become boring.

In the worksheet we work our way toward creating a Forgiveness Declaration that we then use, at least once per day for a week or more. If the issue is a larger one we could use the Forgiveness Declaration for a month, or even the traditional time often set for such inner work of forty days. The suggestion of a week is the minimum unless you get an obvious and definite sense of completion.

Four Steps to Forgiveness

The Forgiveness Declaration is made up of four sentences, which cover each of the four steps to forgiveness. The declaration can be used for any kind of issue, big or small. It's best to start with relatively small issues the first few times until we get the idea.

The four steps to forgiveness:

STEP 1: State who you need to forgive and for what.
STEP 2: Acknowledge what you need to release to allow yourself to forgive.
STEP 3: State the benefits you will get from forgiving.
STEP 4: Commit yourself to forgiving.

A typical Forgiveness Declaration looks like this:

1. I am willing to forgive John for avoiding me.
2. I now choose to release my feelings of sadness, anger and fear. (You can choose to do additional emotional release too.)
3. I acknowledge that forgiving John benefits me, as I will feel happier, healthier and more peaceful.
4. I commit myself to forgiving John and I accept the peace and freedom which forgiveness brings.

Four Steps To Forgiveness WORKSHEET

1. Who and What

Think about the person you need to forgive and why you need to forgive them and enter the details below:

I want to forgive _____ for _____.

This creates a sentence about who you need to forgive and what you need to forgive them for.

Examples:

- I want to forgive Janet for stealing my boyfriend.
- I want to forgive John for hitting me when I was a child.
- I want to forgive my father for not loving me enough.

2. Release Possible Blocks

Write a sentence about any feelings which may be in the way of you forgiving this situation, such as anger, pain, fear, envy, wanting vengeance and so on.

I now choose to release my feelings of _____

Make a sentence out of a list of painful feelings you still have about what happened in the past:

Examples:

- I now choose to release my feelings of anger and fear.
- I now choose to release my feelings of hatred, bitterness and resentment.
- I now let go of my feelings of sadness, pain, and misery.

3. Benefits

List the reasons you want to be able to forgive and then create a sentence out of these. What benefits would you get from forgiving them? How would you feel, how would your attitude be better? How would your behaviour be different? This helps to strengthen your desire and motivation to forgive.

Make a sentence with a list of benefits you will obtain from forgiving. Do this by completing the sentence below with a list of the feelings that you expect to have once you have forgiven. Preferably state positive feelings rather than lack of negative feelings ("more peaceful" rather than "less fearful").

I acknowledge that forgiving this situation will benefit me,

as I will feel _____

Examples:

- I acknowledge that forgiving my mother benefits me, as I will feel happier, healthier and more peaceful.
- I see that forgiving John benefits me, as I will feel free, loving and able to get on with my life.

4. Commitment

Create a sentence to affirm and confirm your intention to forgive.

I commit myself to forgiving _____ [person] and I accept the peace and freedom which forgiveness brings.

In this sentence you declare your intention to forgive the person and affirm your choice to live life from a wiser and higher perspective.

Example:

- I commit to forgiving Janet and I accept the peace and freedom which forgiveness brings.

Build Your Forgiveness Declaration

You now build a Forgiveness Declaration by combining the sentences you created above.

Example 1:

- I want to forgive Janet for stealing my boyfriend.
- I now choose to release my feelings of bitterness and resentment.

- I acknowledge that forgiveness benefits me, as I will feel happier, healthier and more peaceful.
- I commit myself to forgiving Janet and I accept the peace and freedom which forgiveness brings.

Example 2:

- I want to forgive my father for not loving me enough.
- I now choose to release my feelings of anger, disappointment and resentment.
- I acknowledge that forgiveness benefits me, as I will feel free, loving and more alive.
- I commit myself to forgiving my father and I accept the peace and freedom which forgiveness brings.

PRACTICE

Choose how long you will work with your Forgiveness Declaration (7 days, 21 days, etc) and at what times(s) of the day you will use it. Say it at least three times either out loud or quietly in your mind in each session. If it feels right you can keep repeating the Declaration for 5 or 10 minutes.

As you repeat the Declaration you may notice that your feelings will change (i.e., in Step 2 anger changes to frustration and so on). If this happens, just change your wording to match your actual feelings in the moment as best you can.

As part of freeing yourself of old feelings, you may need to do other kinds of emotional release such as talking things over with a friend or even seeing a therapist. As you work with this, you may find unexpected feelings and long forgotten memories arise. Just let them pass or find support if you need it. If you believe in a higher power it is only natural you want that to be part of your Forgiveness Declaration. Simply add a sentence at the end such as, "I ask God's help in forgiving and in becoming free," or "I invite and accept God's grace in helping me to forgive."

PART TWO

Blocks to Forgiveness

High Ideals and Gut Feelings

To be able to forgive we must first meet the legitimate needs of the parts of us that don't want to.

You will notice that we started by looking at the benefits to practising forgiveness. Our ideals about forgiveness are not likely to connect with our gut level feelings where a lot of our forgiving needs to happen. Looking at the benefits of becoming more forgiving helps bridge the gap between our ideals and our gut feelings and allows forgiveness to happen much more easily. We need to fully accept our gut feelings about those we want to forgive before we can move into genuine forgiveness. Acceptance of our feelings may mean that we need to go through a process of releasing those feelings before we can move on.

Sometimes we need to do more than just release the feelings, we may need to honour them too. It may be that we really need to listen to our own feelings and take them more fully into account. Our gut feelings may be offering us some basic wisdom about a person or situation. If we have a feeling in our belly to not trust someone, then that may very well be right. We need to take that feeling on board or we could be blocked in our attempts to forgive. It may just mean that we can forgive the person, but need to see real evidence of a change before we will trust them again.

It is better not to attempt reconciliation with someone who we have a bad feeling about. We override such a feeling at our peril. If we override our feelings, by trying to push ourselves into forgiving someone before we are really ready, we risk being harmed by them again. Also, we could be damaging our relationship with ourselves by not trusting our own feelings. We need to combine the wisdom of our high ideals with the wisdom of our gut feelings to truly forgive.

Brow beating ourselves into "forgiving" someone before we have really dealt with the underlying emotions that we feel about them is not genuine forgiveness;

it is false forgiveness (see later chapter on *False Forgiveness*). We are also then likely to reconcile with someone who may well hurt us again. This would not benefit us, or the person we are trying to forgive. If we re-establish a relationship with someone who is very likely to cause us further harm (and who has not shown genuine remorse or genuine change in behaviour or attitudes) that has more to do with foolishness than forgiveness. True forgiveness brings freedom, lightness and happiness; false forgiveness brings enmeshment, dependency and usually more misery.

Sometimes we are in a hurry to forgive because we hope that will take away the pain or distress we are feeling. Sometimes we are in a hurry to forgive because we want to get away from the rage, hate and anger churning inside us. Sometimes we are in a hurry to forgive because we cannot bear any kind of conflict. This is all understandable, but it is not helpful. It is important not to rush the process if we are to genuinely forgive and not recreate the same or similar circumstances all over again – possibly with the same person.

As we learn to reconcile our high ideals with our gut feelings we become more reconciled with ourselves. We may have assumed that the part of us that does not want to forgive is "bad". The logic goes, "Forgiveness is good, so the part of me which does not want to forgive must be bad." This is fundamentally faulty logic, as we cannot become more forgiving by being judgmental and blaming towards ourselves.

An exercise in self-blame and self-judgement, by assuming that part of us is bad, does not lead us to becoming more forgiving. It just leads to us being split within ourselves and feeling guilty because we are not as forgiving as we "should" be.

We need to explore the part of us that is not ready to forgive, and uncover its legitimate needs so that we can respond to them. It may be that we are actually ready to forgive, but not ready to re-establish a relationship with the other person. In some cases we may need to categorically commit ourselves to not having anything more to do with the person unless we see very definite signs of change in their attitude and behaviour. We may need to make this kind of commitment to ourselves before we can forgive them and before we can forgive ourselves for getting into the situation in the first place.

We also need to explain to our gut-level self the benefits of forgiveness in terms to which it can relate. Many of us have heard of the benefits of forgiveness in terms of it being a good thing to do, a merciful thing to do, a compassionate thing to do, and so on. We may believe that we will have a better place in heaven, or earn good karma, from forgiving. This is all very well, but it is unlikely to have much effect if part of us is holding a deep grudge, has taken an extreme dislike to someone, or is really resentful.

Our gut level may want to know, "If forgiveness is so great then what is in it for me?" It is vitally important to understand that we are the person who benefits the most when we forgive. Yet, we need to know why this is true and not just hold it as an idea in our heads. If we are not truly aware of the benefits we gain by forgiving a part of us may hold out and refuse to forgive. This can cause us to become divided within ourselves if we feel we should forgive, but simply cannot. Of course we then need to forgive ourselves our inability to forgive! But if we are confused about it, and cannot even look at the issue, then there is little chance of that happening.

There is a way we can reach the parts of us that resist forgiving and help those parts be more ready to forgive. There is no need to rely on some far away ideal or the promise of an eventual distant heavenly state to justify forgiveness. There is no point in trying to convince ourselves to forgive when we are not ready yet, and it is not necessary to do so anyway. Once we clearly see the benefits which forgiveness brings, we will do it because we genuinely want to even at a gut level. The gut level part of us and the high-minded idealistic part of us will come more into alignment and forgiveness will become much more natural and easy.

Try this:

1. Think of someone you want to forgive, but have not been able to do so. What, at your gut level, stops you forgiving them?

2. What harmless, healthy, and life-enhancing things can you do for yourself to make it easier for you to forgive them?

Be Wounded, or be Wise

*When we forgive we turn painful lesions
into useful lessons.*

Do we want to stay wounded or do we want to be wise? We only gain in wisdom if we actually learn from our experiences. Yet, we are unlikely to gain any wisdom, or helpful insights, from an experience if we are too wounded to feel anything other than bitterness and resentment about it.

We need to be willing to release painful feelings around an event to fully gain the benefits, which are available from it. We may wonder what possible benefit we can obtain from a particularly painful event; however, we could turn this around and decide that the more painful the event the more important it is to derive some benefit out of it. A benefit is good, no matter how small. The ability to find a benefit, or derive meaning, from an event can have a profound effect on our healing process, as it reconnects us with what is good in life and what is good in ourselves.

If we hold onto our wounds in an area of life then we hold back the growth of wisdom in that area too. If we stay wounded, and do not engage with the forgiveness process, we are less likely to have the necessary wisdom to avoid or prevent similar types of painful events. Even if a painful sense of aversion stops us from creating exactly the same type of situation with the same person, we may stumble into similar experiences, as we will be running blind.

When we hold on tightly to a painful experience we are holding ourselves hostage to that pain. Have you ever met a person who is so embittered by something that it is hard to reach them? Bitterness is not exactly passive is it? It spills out all over the place and can affect the people around the embittered person. People who get locked into, "They did this to me," and who do not get past that, then go on to do similar things to others. Bitterness makes people abusive, and it make them assume that their abusiveness is justified as they feel that they are the "victim". Alternatively it makes them so withdrawn that they are unavailable to

41

connect with in a healthy way. If we had a parent, teacher, or carer like this, it can be very damaging.

If we feel bitter it is important to know that bitterness is an active and harmful process of thinking and feeling. Bitter and resentful people as parents are unable to give their children the love they need. Bitter and resentful bosses are unable to support their staff. Bitter people go after "the money" and do not care about much else, as they feel uncared for and can only connect with others who are the same. Most of us tend to avoid a bitter person – which gives them something else to be bitter about. It is vital to release bitter wounds and step into the wisdom, which is awakened through forgiveness. If we want to have a happy and healthy life then forgiveness is essential; it is not optional.

●●●●●

Forgiveness is not something separate and distinct from such things as wisdom, insight or emotional intelligence. Forgiveness particularly has a lot to do with developing wisdom. A more forgiving attitude makes it easier to develop wisdom, as we are more able to look beyond our own initial reactions and look deeper. We may then see that what was going on with the other person was nothing to do with us and was them acting out some pain or fear of their own. Likewise a deeper capacity for wisdom makes it easier to forgive. It makes us more understanding of other people and their motive and less likely that we will take things personally.

Wisdom is, in part, our capacity to extract meaning and value from our experiences. The more capacity we have to extract meaning from an experience the more likely that we see ways in which good will come out of it. This makes it easier to forgive. Wisdom is not an abstract quality as it brings very practical benefits in handling even very tricky situations.

Situations in our life which may seem like complex mazes, and difficult or impossible to get out of when we are stuck in them, can be easily handled when we have a view from above. When we see a maze from above it is easy to see the way out. Wisdom lets us see the mazes we confront in our lives from above and lets us see the simple answer, which may have been right in front of us.

When I was about ten years old I lived in a rough area in Glasgow, Scotland where there were many street gangs. Some of the gangs were loyal to two soccer teams, Celtic and Rangers, and there was fierce and extreme rivalry between them. The Celtic and Rangers fans very often had violent clashes that were reported in the local news. As I was walking home from school one day I was suddenly surrounded by a gang who demanded to know, "What team do you support, Celtic or Rangers!" I saw no clue as to the right answer as none of them were wearing team colours, so at first I did not know what to say. I did know that it would not be a good idea to give the wrong answer, as I would probably get beat up.

Then I suddenly knew what to answer and how to say it. I loudly proclaimed, "I support Scotland!" As that was the name of our national team, they cheered enthusiastically and I walked away before they could think of something else to make trouble about.

This kind of resolution to a situation comes from the natural wisdom of our forgiving mind. The forgiving mind thinks "outside of the box" and is not constrained by the limits placed on it by others. It naturally looks for win/win solutions no matter what the problem. It looks to ennoble and enhance, and to help and to heal. Therefore the development of forgiveness, which leads to the development of our natural wisdom, not only helps us handle our wounds, it helps us prevent further wounds happening in the first place. It helps us handle crises, make better choices and create better relationships.

We have the capacity to transform what could have turned out to be ugly and painful experiences into something much more positive for all concerned, or at least get through them relatively unscathed. When we listen to the part of us that wants to offer forgiveness and accept forgiveness, such transformation becomes more accessible to us. We become more the author of our experience.

If we have not forgiven, other things masquerading as wisdom may take its place. Attitudes like, "People can't be trusted," "Men are just impossible," and the like, fill the void and set us up for more difficulty in the future. Such attitudes are lesions not lessons: they are wounds not wisdom. Our true lessons bring a sense of freedom and lightness not a sense of restriction and heaviness.

Unforgiveness is the regular and ongoing maintenance of an old pain. If someone hits us with a stick and we then pick up the same stick and strike ourselves with it ten times, who has hurt us the most? It is obviously our own action that is hurting us the most. Yet that is what we do when we stay in a state of unforgiveness; we are hitting ourselves with our assailant's stick – many times, often for years.

Imagine we had a meter that clocked up how much pain we were in and for how long (like an electric meter for pain), let's call it the Painometer. Whereas an electric meter measures kilowatt-hours, the Painometer measures pain-I-got hours.

The original event may be, say, one pain-I-got hour. How many units of pain do we clock up every time we have angry or upset thoughts about the event? Over months and years we could clock up many times more pain than caused by the original event. We could be turning an event that caused us only one pain-I-got hour into ten or a hundred pain-I-got hours. If the other person intended to hurt us we are helping them by doing a better job than they did! If they did not intend to hurt us there is even less reason to be hurting ourselves needlessly.

When we plaintively cry, "Why did this happen?," what we might really mean is, "Why did this happen to me?" Life is a package deal, we get hard times and we get easy times. If we cling to the hard times even during the easy times we only have ourselves to blame for the resulting misery. It may be that we are holding onto the pain as a reminder (as if it were some kind of fridge magnet) so that we can prevent the same painful thing happening again, but totally the opposite is true.

It is by forgiving we ensure it is less likely to happen again, because as we get above the maze and can better recognize and avoid similar situations. Besides, holding onto a pain so that we will not create that pain again makes no sense. It would be the same as if an unwelcome visitor comes to our house and we refuse to let them leave so that they won't come again!

We have all had situations that would have turned out better if we had handled them more wisely. These situations may seem to have nothing to do with the situations we have not yet forgiven, but they are actually closely linked. Any forgiveness process we engage in improves our relationships with all the people in our life. By forgiving anyone we get better relationships with everyone. Each step in the path of forgiveness helps us tap more readily into our innate wisdom and helps us make the most out of our relationships with the people we meet and the situations we experience. At the very least being more forgiving will help us become a more happy and pleasant person to be around. We will be less prone to the moods and attitudes that have a negative or annoying effect on others. By forgiving we become less wounded and wiser.

Try this:

1. Can you see situations where you can turn wounds into wisdom or lesions into lessons?

2. Have a look as the definitions below of both unforgiveness and of forgiveness. If one of these definitions appeals to you maybe make a note of it and put it on your fridge, bathroom mirror, or somewhere private where you can see it regularly.

Unforgiveness is hooking myself into a painful experience.
Unforgiveness is holding on to the pain from the past.
Unforgiveness is being unkind to myself.

Unforgiveness is saying "No" to life.
Unforgiveness is not trusting myself and not trusting the deeper processes of life.
Unforgiveness is not allowing myself to be bigger than life's events.
Unforgiveness is not allowing myself to grow from the events of my life.

Forgiveness is unhooking myself from a painful experience.
Forgiveness is letting go of the pain from the past.
Forgiveness is being kind to myself.
Forgiveness is saying "Yes" to life.
Forgiveness is trusting myself and trusting the process of life.
Forgiveness is allowing myself to be bigger than life's events.
Forgiveness is allowing myself to grow from the events of my life.
Forgiveness: the act of transforming wounds into wisdom.

Choose to Blame or Choose to Learn

Better to be busy learning than busy blaming.

Blaming, such as blaming Politicians, Men, Women, or some other "them" too much, can stop us seeing how we can improve our situation. Of course there are times when politicians, or whoever, gets it wrong and need to be challenged. However, if blaming becomes habitual and compulsive it keeps us in a negative frame of mind. Releasing blame and replacing it with our ability to learn helps to create a more forgiving climate in our inner world.

If we think about people we know who are Blamers we may notice that they do not tend to learn much from their experiences. Their focus is on what they believe others need to do differently and not on what they themselves need to do differently. They are busy blaming everyone and everything and there is not much space inside them to grow as a person.

Blamers have many "reasons" why they are "right" and why their feelings are justified. They spend a lot of time polishing up these reasons and adding bits to them so that they get bigger and bigger. The really "smart" Blamers can find amazingly complex and sophisticated arguments to support their attitude, but it all just boils down to, "I am not happy and it is their/his/her/God's fault."

People living on Blame Street think a friend is someone who helps them to stay miserable. We are not allowed to be their friend unless we agree with their unhappy way of thinking. If we were to disagree with their reasons for being unhappy they could get very angry with us. It would be as if we tried to take away their favourite toy. They might even hate us and think we are an enemy

Blame is a slippery slope to misery. The more we express blame the more we need to defend our position to bolster it. The more we defend our blaming attitudes the more we are defending our right to be a victim. Yet, if we want to stop blaming we may feel that we are faced with a terrible alternative: to turn the blame inwards and blame ourselves instead. This is a horrifying prospect and one we naturally want to avoid. Yet that is how blame works, it wants to go somewhere.

The real answer is to stop blaming altogether. Working from the principle that it is better to redirect energy rather than just trying to stop it, we can redirect blaming energy into learning. Redirecting our attention by asking ourselves questions helps us shift the energy of blame into something useful and constructive.

How can this situation help me learn and grow? How can I handle this challenge so that I feel empowered? How can I let my happiness come from inside and be more independent of things which are external?

One area of learning is to look at how others mirror our own attitudes back to us. People often treat us the way we treat ourselves. Our demeanour, body language and tone of voice say a lot about us. What we do not say speaks as much about us as what we say. If we are highly critical of ourselves and don't treat ourselves kindly, then it is not surprising if others copy our example. A few kindly souls will treat us better than our attitude warrants, but these are the exceptions.

Depending on our character, we may become quieter around loud people; or we may become louder. We may become pushy around people who are resisting doing what we want and we may become resistant around pushy people. Likewise other people will tend to change their behaviour to match our attitudes and character.

There does not seem to be anything particularly unusual about the fact in a relationship, or in a team, one person may seem like an optimist while another may seem like a pessimist. Yet, one could simply be emphasising their role to offer a balance to the attitudes of the other. The attitudes and behaviour that we are blaming someone for, may be in response to our attitudes and behaviour.

Two owners of a company I once worked for gave very different answers when I asked how it went when they had a meeting with a major client. One told me, "It went great!" while the other said, "Oh, there are problems!" Later the "pessimistic" one confessed to me that he was fed up playing the role of "nae sayer", but felt he had to or the other owner would run the company into the ground. I suggested that they were unconsciously balancing each other (the Balance Dance as I like to call it) and that if he switched roles the other owner would have to switch roles too.

When they returned from the next meeting with the client I asked them how it went. The normally pessimistic one spoke first and said, "It went great! They want to expand the project…" then the other owner quickly interrupted him….

"Wait a minute. Let's not get carried away here. There are issues that need to be worked out...." I nearly fell off my chair in surprise about how well my advice worked. The normally optimistic one had to switch his role because the pessimistic one had switched his.

We may be tempted to become more extreme than we normally feel in order to make a point with someone. Yet this usually just complicates the situation and causes them to act more extremely. I have two friends who are at slightly different sides of the political spectrum. Their attitudes are fairly mild when I talk to them. Yet when they talk about politics with each other they soon end up arguing. They get into blaming and accusing each other, turning into extremists who I can hardly recognize as being the same people.

•••••

Life is a mirror, often quite literally. The people around us may be showing us our imbalances by acting out the other extreme. If we insist in blaming them we will miss the lessons and insights we can gain. If we find ourselves wanting to blame someone, we could try taking a step back from the situation and see if there is some kind of Balance Dance going on. We can look to see if behaviour we don't like in someone else has to do with them reacting to behaviour or attitudes which they see in us. If we show lack of commitment in a relationship the other person may feel it and show lack of commitment too (or they could go the other way and get "clingy"). Instead of blaming them for their behaviour we could make a stronger commitment – if it is a relationship we really want. Even if it still does not work out we will be stronger as we chose to learn and to grow rather than being stuck on blaming.

The more we can let go of our tendency to blame the more easily forgiving will come to us. Focusing on learning and growing instead of blaming creates a spaciousness where healthy thoughts and feelings can become established. We are then focused on that which is life enhancing and life giving.

Try this:

1. Can you see where letting go of blame would make it easier for you to forgive?

2. Can you see any situations in which you may be in a Balance Dance with someone where you are unconsciously trying to balance each other out? What would happen if you changed your attitude and behaviour around them?

Aversions

When we avoid too much we live in a void too much.

When our unforgiving mind is active we can build up aversions to particular people. This can cause us to avoid the places where these people go and can cause us to constrain and limit our work or social life. Of course, sometimes avoiding someone can be a wise thing to do as it gives us a chance to have some breathing space. However, it can also interfere with us doing what we need to. Also it can get in the way of us learning and growing in ways that could be good for us.

I asked a friend of mine, Robert, if he ever went to a local choir, as I knew he was interested in singing. He said, "No I never go as Janet sometimes goes there and I want to avoid her." When asked why he avoided her he told me he once thought of her as a close friend, but when he really needed support, just after his mother died, she went out of her way to avoid him. He felt very badly let down and did not want to even see her. It turned out that he had not told Janet how he felt. He was passing her in the street without talking to her in the hope that she would "get the message".

The problem with Robert's reaction is that throwing mud into a pool does not make it clearer. His attempts to "tell" Janet how he felt by ignoring her simply confused the issue. I knew Janet well enough to be able to see that she was not the kind of stable, solid person who could be relied on in times of crises. Robert could choose to accept Janet the way she is and keep the parts of the relationship that work. However, he felt that her behaviour meant that she was not a friend, as she did not do what he believed friends "should" do. He went even further, as he was trying to punish her, by ignoring her in public. Robert's behaviour hurt and confused Janet. She was basically well-intentioned, but simply did not have the internal strength to support someone through a crisis.

Another problem with Robert's reaction is that it limited his social life and caused him to miss out on things he wanted. He really wanted to join the choir, but could not let himself, just because Janet went to it. This kind of behaviour feeds on itself. Refusing to forgive someone and then having to avoid them, limits and constrains us. It can become a habit and it then becomes difficult for us to create genuine connection with others, as we will all too easily put them on our "avoid" list.

It is one thing to avoid someone who is deliberately harmful to us; it is another to avoid someone who is basically well meaning, but who just does not behave how we think they should.

Janet is a kind person who has not properly dealt with her own painful experiences. This makes it hard for her to cope with other people's pain. She probably felt overwhelmed and had no idea how to support Robert around the death of his mother. Robert is also a normally kind person, but he just did not understand Janet's limitations.

The cause of someone's behaviour can be the opposite of what we assume. To Robert it looked like Janet was being insensitive when in fact she was overly sensitive. She cannot handle the pain of people she cares about. Ironically her non-support was a sign that she cared, not that she did not care. Robert's reaction confused her and fed into her feelings of shame and inadequacy.

Even if we decide it is better to avoid someone we do not need to create and maintain negative beliefs about them. We can decide, "This person is not right for me just now," and bless them on their way. Similarly we do not need to label ourselves either, we are just not going to get on well with everyone.

In handling our aversions and our sensitivity issues we may end up going to the other extreme and play out brash and bold behaviour. A situation may seem too much for us and yet we may feel forced to cope. We may be tempted to use alcohol or drugs to help us cope with the things we would rather avoid. Yet, that does not resolve anything. We can learn the skills to handle the situations and the people we avoid, if it seems wise to so do. The first step is admitting to ourselves that we have a genuine aversion to someone or some situation, or that we have a sensitivity issue going on.

Try this:

1. Is there something you like to do, which is important to you, but you don't because you are avoiding someone? How could you use forgiveness to help the situation?

2. Have you ever felt that you are "too sensitive" and felt shame or guilt about it? Is there a way you can now let those feelings go?

False Forgiveness

We may not be sure our feelings are right,
but we sure have the right to our feelings.

False forgiveness looks like the real thing, but is not genuine. We can detect False Forgiveness by noticing what is going on in our body. False forgiveness has a sense of tightness, heaviness, rigidity and hardness; it does not bring the good feelings of genuine forgiveness. Genuine forgiveness brings a sense of lightness, of ease, and of letting go. Genuine forgiveness may also bring a feeling that any harm has somehow been "undone". It is as if the whole thing had never happened, yet we are somehow better than before. False forgiveness binds us to unhappy experiences; true forgiveness sets us free.

False forgiveness may hide itself under different masks such as a condescending attitude, denial or repression. The things we say to ourselves which are False Forgiveness may sound like:

"They are pathetic, but I forgive them."
"I don't care about him, so he did not hurt me."
"I knew that she would do something stupid like that, so I have nothing to forgive."
"I know better than they do."
"I never wanted him/her anyway, so he/she did not reject me."
"I have forgiven them, so there is nothing more to say about it."

If we have low self-esteem we may let people get away with too much. We may dismiss our need for the other person to make amends, or to show genuine remorse, because we are not sure that our feelings are right. If so, we need to bear this in mind: we may not be sure our feelings are right, but we sure have the right to our feelings. If we do not acknowledge our own feelings we may allow ourselves to become reconciled with someone without any real forgiveness taking place. We need to treat our feelings with respect otherwise we may find that other people will not respect our feelings either.

If we are not connected with our feelings then true forgiveness is not possible. Allowing our feelings to surface clears the way for us to reconnect with ourselves so that forgiveness can happen. With False Forgiveness we try and avoid connecting with our feelings; with genuine forgiveness we honour our feelings and respect them, and then we let them go or take healthy action based on them.

When dealing with a deep issue, we may find that tears well up, or that anger surfaces. It helps to say a kindly "yes" to whatever feelings arise so that we can let go and release. If we push down our feelings, with a "No!" reaction, this can create a coldness or numbness inside us

With genuine forgiveness our tears, or our anger, will come with a sense of yielding or softness. This brings healing and openness rather than a hardness or brittleness that comes with False Forgiveness. With False Forgiveness we create a split within ourselves as we are blocking out the parts of us that need to be healed. Our hurts need to be healed, or be in process of being healed, for us to genuinely forgive.

If we numb out our feelings we cut ourselves off from our inner knowing of when someone is genuinely remorseful and when they are just trying to manipulate us. If we are cut off from ourselves, we may mistake someone's fear of repercussions for genuine remorse. When we are connected with ourselves we know when our gut feeling is telling us not to trust someone because they are not genuinely sorry. We will be able to receive any warnings from inside ourselves that the person is only temporarily afraid and that they will be back to their old ways soon enough.

We do not want to let ourselves be bullied or pushed into "forgiving", as it can only lead to False Forgiveness. No one has the right to demand that we forgive them. People who are habitually pushy tend to push for everything they want including forgiveness. We need to allow ourselves the time we need, as we cannot forgive on cue to fit in with someone's schedule. We cannot even forgive to our own schedule as forgiveness is not an act of will.

If we are wary of conflict, we might tell someone that we forgive them "for the sake of peace". It is not true peace as we have just been scared, bullied, or cajoled into False Forgiveness. We are not really doing anyone a favour, in diminishing ourselves by offering a false peace.

In order to forgive someone we may need them to fully hear how we feel. A genuinely remorseful person will want to hear us out even though it may be hard for them to bear the guilt it will bring up. Having a neutral third person present can be a big help. It is much easier to forgive when we can see that we are being respected. We may even find that the issue was largely due to a misunderstanding rather than any intention to hurt us.

Although we want to avoid False Forgiveness, acting as if we forgive someone can help make it real. By acting the part we can end up forgiving them even when we did not really mean to. Many of us have experienced this as kids when well-meaning parents or teachers would push us into shaking hands or making up with someone we had just been fighting with. Afterwards we find that we have forgiven them after all. Feeling that we are both in the same boat (having parents or teachers hassling us) made it easier to forgive them. Their willingness to shake hands with us (albeit under pressure) shows that they are not so bad after all, or that they think we are not so bad too.

The difference between False Forgiveness and using the technique of "acting as if" we forgive in order to trigger genuine forgiveness has to do with our intention. False forgiveness means we do not know the forgiveness is not real; with "acting as if" we do know it is not real – at least not yet.

People in a co-dependent relationship may seem to "forgive" their partner, but really it is False Forgiveness. If they truly forgave their partner they would either become immune to their behaviour, or they would walk away from the relationship without malice or ill-will.

When we honour and reclaim our feelings, we reclaim the parts of us that hook us into unhealthy relationships. When those hooks are gone we become freer in our choices. Forgiveness sets us free.

Forgiveness is an act of willingness not an act of will

Forgiveness is not an act of will. We cannot just decide to forgive then it is done. Our conscious decision to forgive merely starts the process. We then need the willingness to see it through and to nurture and support our capacity to forgive to enable it to happen.

Supporting our commitment to forgiving may mean facing things we have been avoiding. This can mean needing to accept painful feelings, releasing anger and allowing our feelings of hatred, bitterness and resentment to surface so we can be free of them.

It can be tempting to bypass painful or uncomfortable feelings. This leads to False Forgiveness, or no forgiveness. It is only in accepting pain that we can heal it. However, we do not have to re-experience the original pain in the same way. We can re-experience the event from a very different perspective.

For example, if we had a painful experience as a child, we do not need to go back into that state as if we were still a child. Instead we can hold the childlike part of us with a feeling of compassion and kindness while we face the experience.

This makes it easier to experience the event, makes it less painful, and makes it easier to forgive.

We are an adult now, and can bring a very different view into the experiences we had before. Now we are older and wiser, we can face unresolved events from our past. We can handle them in new ways by including the greater wisdom, insight and experience that we have now. As adults we hold a mature presence for the younger parts of ourselves to help transform our earlier experiences into wisdom.

Try this:

1. Have you ever pretended to forgive someone in order to "keep the peace"? If so, did it work?

2. Have you ever pretended to forgive someone to avoid handling your own hurt feelings? If so, can you now allow yourself to accept how you really felt?

Irritations and Frustrations

*Practising on the small things makes it easier
to forgive the big things.*

A sense of irritation and frustration may seem like a minor thing. However, when we look closer we see that such feelings cost us a lot as they take away our peace of mind. What is more valuable than happiness and peace of mind? Yet we throw it away for the sake of trivialities like the train being late, the TV being boring, or something not being the way it "should" be. If we really want to be happy let's not give up our chances so easily.

We may be tempted to respond that "they" are making us unhappy and it is not us who are choosing to be that way. Yet in our heart of hearts we know better. We know better than to let the small things bother us, but somehow they do. We may be irritated by someone walking, or driving slowly in front of us, when we want to go faster. We may get frustrated when the mail is late and we are expecting an important letter. We might get annoyed at all the junk messages in our email. There are numerous ways that irritation and frustration can enter into our minds and take away our happiness in the moment.

Do we really want to go through life not being in charge of our own mind? Do we really want our happiness to be dependent so much on things over which we have no control? Do we want our sense of well-being dependent on the rail system, the TV companies, or the generators of spam and scams?

The problem with things that make us unhappy is that we let them take us out of this moment. It may seem that we are unhappy because the post is late, right now, but usually we are unhappy because we are anticipating what it means. We are anticipating something unpleasant in the future so we feel unhappy about that. In those moments we are not actually in this moment, we are in an unhappy future of our own creation based on fearful imaginings. The problem with the future and the past is that they cannot be changed as they are not reachable. It's only in this moment we can do anything. Although we cannot change the situation, and make the post be on time, we can change how we respond to it.

We can change our response to events only when we take responsibility for those responses. If we keep assuming that the problem is "out there" then there is not much we can do. If we assume the responsibility is inside us; that it is up to us to decide how we will respond to events, then we can begin to change our responses more in line with ones which will make it easier for us to maintain our peace of mind and maintain our happiness. It may take a bit of work to break out of our existing patterns and habitual reactions, but each step is a step towards greater happiness and a greater capacity to forgive.

When we can let go of judging the shop worker who is abrupt or rude, not take it personally when a car cuts us off, not get upset when someone takes "our" parking place, and so on, the more easy it gets to release and let go of the bigger issues. By letting go of these irritations and minor offences we get better at living up to our capacity to be in the moment and enjoy life.

There is no point in telling ourselves "I should not get annoyed" and then trying to repress it or ignore it. If we are annoyed, that is just how it is and we need to deal with how it is. We first may need to learn to not get annoyed about getting annoyed and not get irritated about being irritated! If we can notice it with curiosity, "Oh I am annoyed about such and such.... Isn't that interesting," this helps us detach from our reactions and stop adding fuel to them by feeding them with justifications.

Even this simple act of flowing with what is going on inside us, by noticing it rather than repressing, or being caught up in it, can be a powerful step towards a healthy life pattern of self-healing and self-regeneration. This way of learning to handle our feelings by detaching from them takes practice. It is all too easy to slip into being caught up in them or by trying to push them away. We just need to let them be and watch them as they run out of steam. It is a bit like watching a fire as it dies down of its own accord.

With minor things the simple act of taking a few deep breaths can allow us to re-centre ourselves and feel happy again. With more serious situations it may take a dozen deep breaths, or even a hundred deep breaths (maybe sitting down with a cup of tea) so that we can let go. However, distracting ourselves with something else can help a lot with minor irritations.

The more we can let go of the small stuff and minor annoyances the easier it gets to let go of the bigger situations and issues which we face. Sometimes all we can do is to let go and let things take their course. When we practise letting go of things that disturb us we are training ourselves to be more forgiving. We are taking more responsibility for our own thoughts and feelings and being less swayed by others' behaviour or reactions. We are letting go of old habits of thinking and feeling which get in the way of us being able to hold a peaceful and forgiving state of mind.

Try this:

1. Think of a situation in which you might get annoyed or irritated (something not too extreme to begin with). Imagine the situation enough till you feel reactions in your body. Take a few deep breaths to let go of the build up of stress. As the feelings leave you, imagine yourself smiling and being able to take it all in your stride.

Notice how you feel better as the feeling of annoyance or irritation leaves your body and affirm to yourself that you are learning to forgive and to let go of all things, both big and small.

2. Next time you start to react to something ask yourself, "Is it worth giving up my happiness for this?"

Judgement

When we are absolutely sure we are right,
we can be absolutely sure we are wrong.

Judgement can be very tempting, but it fills our mind with disharmony and unhappy thoughts. The effect can vary from a slight sense of disapproval to a more intense form of what I like to call the Machine Gun Mind. The Machine Gun Mind is when the mind systematically works its way round a room and forms harsh judgements of everyone there. This kills any chance – temporarily at least – of creating good connections with the people present. I first noticed the Machine Gun Mind when walking into a classroom as part of a new course I was starting at college.

I looked around the room and my mind turned into a machine as it worked its way round everyone there and immediately made judgements about all of them: *"He looks strange. She looks bitchy. He looks nerdy,"* and so on. Of course, once I got to know the people properly those hasty judgements passed and I made some good friends. If I had gone by the impressions of my Machine Gun Mind I would have been tempted to avoid all of them and just kept to myself.

Judgement is not the same thing as discernment. Judgement carries with it undertones of looking down on someone, of harsh opinions, and of negative feelings. Discernment is a sense of noticing what is right for us at any given time, without being negative or disparaging about whatever we do not want.

Judgement can sneak in at any time and about anything. It can grow and feed on itself if we reinforce it with yet more judgmental thoughts. This can take us from what was initially a mild annoyance into intense rage if we do not catch it on time.

Judgement can fool us into believing we are defending, when we are really attacking. Judgement is an attack on the value and decency of the other person, dressed up as being "right". At its extreme this can lead to acts of evil. It fools people into thinking some horrid thing that they are doing is for the greater good.

It can make us believe that the other person is bad and therefore deserves what we want to do to them.

Many of the great wrongs done throughout history were by people who believed that they were right. This odd quirk of human nature is one of the saddest and yet one of the most hopeful things about us. It is sad because of the blindness it shows; it is hopeful because it shows that even at our worst we want to believe that we are good.

Even the most wicked of historical figures would have been offended to be called "evil" or to have their actions described as such. They listened to the voice of judgement, which can always find justification for doing harm – no matter how absurd and bizarre the "reasons" seem. Judgement causes us to completely lose perspective, but creates the illusion of a clear perspective. When we are infected by judgement we end up with a very narrow and limited view, which is like a form of temporary insanity. Anyone not caught up in our reaction can see the absurdity of it, but we usually cannot till we let go of judgement. This tendency to cause hurt to others under the guise of doing good is something we all need to face and challenge within ourselves.

· · · · ·

I was out in my garden one day and noticed that my neighbour's hedge was overgrown and hanging over into my garden. I started getting annoyed about it and the more I thought about it the more annoyed I got. "Why does he not look after his hedge better. He should show more respect for his neighbours. He is just lazy...."

Although it was a nice day outside, it was not a nice day inside me. I had got myself into a state and was getting more and more filled with anger and bitter thoughts. My thoughts were ruining my day as they were causing bad feelings to churn around inside me. A variety of justifications were coming to mind as to why I "should" feel angry about this. However, the bottom line was, I was making myself unhappy.

Also the judgmental thoughts I was having were not putting me in a frame of mind where I could find a good solution to the problem. That is one of the fundamental problems with a judgmental attitude: it cuts us off from finding creative win/win solutions. It gets us stuck on blame and wanting to make the other person wrong. Judgmental attitudes cause us to react in ways that make problems worse by escalating them. If I had talked to my neighbour from that angry frame of mind it would have likely upset him and put him on the defensive. Getting into an argument with my neighbour might have got him to trim his hedge, but it could have damaged my relationship with him.

I decided to let go of my judgemental thoughts about my neighbour. I just watched my thoughts for a while, which were like some kind of manic inner TV programme, and gradually they subsided. Not long afterwards my neighbour's overhanging hedge, which I had got so annoyed about, surprised me by starting to bloom and looking really nice. I bumped into my neighbour who, without any prompting from me, apologized profusely about the overhanging hedge and promised to do something about it. I said to him, "No, please leave it as it is. Your hedge is the best looking thing in my garden."

My mum lived in sheltered housing for a short while. The walls between the houses were a bit thin and so she could hear the sound of the man next door, who had developed a bad cough. She could hear him coughing at night while lying in her bed. One morning she bumped into this man who said, "I am sorry about all the coughing sounds I am making, but I have a chest infection which I hope will clear up soon." My mum decided to tell a white lie as she felt sorry for the man and knew the cough was causing him more trouble than anyone else. She said, "Cough? What cough? I never heard a thing." The man looked very surprised, but said nothing.

Not long afterwards the grandchildren came to stay with my mum. They were very noisy and she was worried about it disturbing the neighbour. Next time she saw the man she said, "I hope the noise from my grandchildren didn't disturb you." He gives her a big smile and said, "Noise? What noise? I never heard a thing."

Try this:

1. Think of someone you don't approve of and think of all the reasons you don't approve of them. Now notice what that feels like in your body. If you were eating something that made you feel like this, would you keep eating it or throw it away?

2. Have you ever had negative judgements about someone or something only to find out later that you were completely wrong? If so, that is good – as otherwise, judgement is running your life.

I Just Cannot
Forgive Them

*The truth is not a stick with
which to beat yourself.*

What happens if we feel like there is someone we just cannot forgive? Perhaps someone did something so horrid that we cannot conceive of ever forgiving them. If this is the case, then there is no point in being hard on ourselves. It is better to put aside such events and focus on the issues we do feel able to forgive. However, it may also be helpful to remind ourselves of the benefits which we gain from forgiving and that it is we who really benefit from our acts of forgiveness.

It might also help to look at why we do not want to forgive. Perhaps we want them to suffer. What would we get out of them suffering? Do we want vengeance or justice? How much punishment will be enough for us to be able to forgive them? Should they be punished for eternity? As the old joke goes, "Eternity is an awfully long time." Even a million years of punishment would still be a trivial time in terms of eternity. How does it feel inside to want someone to suffer? As noted before, it may well feel so bad that it is really we who are doing the suffering.

Sometimes we want the person who hurt us to feel the same pain we felt. If they knew how much it hurt that would stop them doing the same thing again, is how the thinking goes. Yet that was probably their justification for hurting us. Perhaps we, or someone else, said or did something to them and they are acting out their pain. If we are justified in wanting to cause hurt are they not justified too? Of course we can argue that this is different as we are the innocent one. Yet, everyone assumes that they are the innocent one.

Although it is good to look at why we resist forgiving we cannot push ourselves into actually doing it. Besides, forgiveness is like anything else in that it grows stronger with practice. Better to start on the easy ones and build up from there rather than straining with an issue we are just not ready for yet.

If we cannot forgive someone in particular, at this time, and feel that we "should" be able to, then it is ourselves that we need to forgive. We need to forgive ourselves first before we will have any chance of forgiving the other person. It could also be that we have trouble forgiving someone because we assume that we will need to be reconciled with them too. If so, reading the chapter on Reconciliation can put our mind at rest on that. We can forgive and still decide to have no contact with the person.

Forgiveness is also about doing right by ourselves as well as doing right by others. We need to maintain a good relationship with ourselves and not push, bully or rush ourselves into forgiving when we are just not ready. Respecting our own inner time-frame and our own natural process will allow us to make quicker progress in the long run. The challenges in learning to forgive often come out of the divisions within ourselves. Healing those divisions, by being reconciled with ourselves, is a major step towards being able to forgive. If we are not ready to forgive a particular person, or event, we can choose let it go for now knowing that we will get to it when we are ready.

Try this:

These suggestions will help cultivate our connection with the deeper and wiser part of ourselves that can forgive. It will connect us with the part of ourselves that seeks freedom, healing and resolution. Here are a few suggestions that may help us loosen up and eventually be able to forgive the more difficult ones.

1. Say this to yourself a few times:
    "I acknowledge that I am having difficulty forgiving [name] for [what they did]. I forgive myself for feeling this way and I look forward to when I can forgive them and that event and be free of its effects forever."

Take a few long deep breaths, letting go on the out breath.

2. Notice when you think of a painful event how it feels in your body. How would it feel to let the pain go and not ever be bothered with it again? How would it feel to have the wisdom and insight to rise above that event? How would your life be better when you are free of the effects of that experience?

Cynicism

Cynicism is the ability to create a better world –
stuck in reverse.

I've come to believe that one of the biggest traps in life, at least for those of us who are thinking types, is cynicism. Cynicism is a bad tempered guard dog, which keeps biting its owner. The owner does not usually even know that it is their own cynical attitude, which keeps hurting them. One of the problems with cynicism is that it masks itself as a winning attitude, but it is really a losing attitude as it keeps us focused on what is "wrong".

When we feel cynical we assume the worst of other people's motives and have "a sneering disbelief" which causes us to assume other's actions are motivated by selfishness, or self-seeking of some kind. If you wonder, "What's wrong with that?" or can relate to it in any way, then this section is for you.

Cynicism is not the same as questioning, doubting or being sceptical. If we are just sceptical we have an open mind, but just need more proof. If we are cynical we have already made up our mind about human nature and what motivates people and have decided that most people's motives are bad or selfish. Cynicism goes beyond doubting or being sceptical as the cynic has made up their mind already. The problem with cynicism is the emotional tone that comes with it. The feelings behind cynicism tend towards bitterness and contempt. A cynical attitude is not a recipe for a happy life and for creating healthy relationships.

Once we start to get cynical we tend to find it easier to find more things to be cynical about. Cynicism is a victim stance towards life. It may not be obvious that it is a victim stance, because it is an aggressive victim stance. It is a pre-emptive strike against the world. If we become cynical we become a clever victim, with many "facts" to support our attitude, but we are still playing the victim. The cynical mind holds itself in readiness, and well prepared, for the next unhappy event, which it fully expects to come round the corner at any moment. If nothing appears, then it can soon make something up.

Cynicism masks its true nature by offering us a false sense of security. It looks like it is protecting us from harm by preventing us from making mistakes. It tells us, "Think the worst of people and they can't take advantage of you." What it does not tell us is that the more we think the worst of people the more we become an unpleasant person to be around. The more good-natured the other person the less they will want to be around us when we are cynical. We are then more likely to attract other cynics instead. We become a magnet for crooks, scammers and dodgy sales people who will pick up on our negative attitude and try to use our fears to manipulate us.

Rather than protecting us from mistakes, cynicism is one of the ultimate mistakes. If we allow an experience to make us cynical it stops us from getting the wisdom and skill we could have got from the experience. Cynicism freezes us out of learning from our experiences and when we stop learning, we stop growing.

What can cause us to become cynical? It could be, being let down, people not understanding what we are trying to achieve, or just being disappointed and bitter about life. We try to protect ourselves from further harm by being on our guard. It could be that we are an idealistic person and have had our ideals shattered by people not living up to what we hoped. We become cynical to protect ourselves from disappointment, or from being misjudged. Yet if we are bitter about human nature, or about a particular group of human beings, then this shows that we feel wounded somewhere. If we are simply wary, and a bit sceptical that is not a sign of a wounded feeling. However, feeling bitter and contemptuous is a sign of a wound and a sign that forgiveness and reconciliation needs to happen. We especially need to become reconciled with ourselves.

Cynicism is a sign of a split between our idealism and our practicality. We have ideals, but we are judging them and dismissing them – just as we judge and dismiss others who are trying to live by their ideals. In reducing others motives to the lowest level, and considering their actions as unworthy, we reduce our own motives to the lowest level too. Cynicism causes us to refuse to express the parts of us that have worthy goals and want us to take worthy action.

If we dismiss our highest motives with, *"You just can't trust people,"* *"No one else will join in,"* *"They will just think I'm an idiot,"* before we even try, then we are choosing to live in fear. It is fear; fear of being misunderstood, fear of being judged, fear of being taken advantage of, fear of looking foolish, which is really behind cynicism. It is only when we express the part of us which wants to leave the world a better place that we find our true place in the world. We can get away with holding back that part of ourselves for a while, but sooner or later we will pay a high price for so doing. If life feels bitter and empty it is because we have become bitter and empty, by refusing the goodness within us a way to be in the world.

If we are maintaining a cynical attitude we are simply acting out old pains and justifying them rather than healing them. We turn our idealism into a weapon and instead of looking to what good can be achieved, we look to what doubtful motives we can assume on the part of those who are trying to achieve it. If we are wary of trusting, that is fine. In some situations that may well be wise.

However, mentally or verbally disparaging someone and deciding in advance that they are bad or that their motives are bad is a form of attack. If we have wide-scale cynicism this is a form of attack on all of humanity, which obviously includes ourselves, so we end up being cynical about ourselves too. Our denial of our own goodness, out of fear of the consequences of expressing it, makes us want to deny it in others too.

If we believe that nobody has much good in them, then we either have to decide that we do not have much good in us either, or we have to decide that we are different and separate from the rest of the human race. Either attitude creates a barrier between us and the rest of humanity and this is what makes cynicism so poisonous.

• • • • •

To break out of patterns of cynicism we need to look at the underlying causes within ourselves. We need to express our capacity to achieve good in the world; yet do so in ways that are realistic and protect us from reasonably avoidable harm. By forgiving those we feel hurt by and becoming reconciled between our need to create good and the fear which blocks us from going ahead, we can then switch our focus from cynical thoughts and responses to life-enhancing ones.

The forgiving mind is not naive. We can learn to trust that there is a basic goodness in people; yet, still make wise provisions for dealing with those who might not live up to it. We can like people, yet still insist on having clear contracts with anyone we do business with. We can trust our life partner; yet still want clear agreements that underpin that trust. We may sometimes be let down, but we learn, make adjustments and move on without getting bitter about it.

Trust and communication are opposite sides of the same coin. The quality of one depends on the quality of the other. High quality of trust creates high quality of communication. Likewise high quality communication creates a high quality of trust. By being willing to learn constructive and life enhancing attitudes our verbal and non-verbal communication will improve. People will become more trusting of us and more willing to connect with us. The quality of our lives is largely dependent on the quality of our relationships. It is only with the help of others that we achieve our goals.

Letting go of cynical attitudes and beliefs gives us a chance to see the goodness in others and the goodness in life. It also gives others a chance to see the goodness in us and to help us express it.

Try this:

1. Are you wary of people? Do you feel that people are basically good or basically bad?
2. Do you expect people to let you down? If so, how can you communicate what you want differently so that you are much more likely to be happy with the outcome?

Guilt and Company

*Much of what happens in life
is emotion disguised as reason.*

It is easier to give if we feel we have plenty. It is easier to forgive if we feel good about ourselves and good about life. It is also easier to forgive if we feel forgiven. If emotions such as guilt, shame, fear and anger become habitual they can make it hard for us to forgive as they distort how we see life and events. It is easier to interpret things negatively if these feelings hold sway. By being more aware of the effect those feelings have on us we are more able to prevent them from dominating us.

If we feel guilt it means that we have acted in ways that have offended our sense of what is right. We have gone against our values and may feel the need to make amends. Guilt can also bring up fear. We may feel afraid of being found out, or afraid of being punished. We may fear possible repercussions, such as someone taking revenge on us. We may either want to hide somewhere or feel compelled to offer restitution, or to find a way to make up for what we did.

We may even want to be punished so that we can get over our guilt. Indeed we might already be punishing ourselves by denying ourselves things we want, or making life harder than it needs to be. Guilt is a painful feeling which isolates us from others, so in some ways guilt is itself a form of punishment.

Guilt can become self-perpetuating. If it moves into fear it can perpetuate itself by becoming our guilty secret, which we have to hide from the world. Having a dark secret, which we hide, makes us feel more guilty and more fearful. We end up bending the truth or telling lies to maintain our secret – then feel guilty about that too.

If guilt moves into anger it perpetuates itself by causing us to hit out in defence and then we feel even more guilt. Someone says something in the "wrong" way, or at the "wrong" moment and we react and blurt something out which we feel bad about. When we are guilty and fearful it is all too easy to feel like we are under attack, even when this is not the case. If the other person reacts and comes back at us with similar behaviour we may assume that this is "proof" that they were trying to attack us, when it was really a misunderstanding. Guilt can create habitual fear or anger. When fuelled by guilt either of these tend to create more of the same and more guilt.

Unresolved feelings of guilt make it harder for us to forgive, as we may not feel that we have anything to offer. It can also affect us in the opposite way and we feel obliged to forgive, to make amends for some wrong we have done. This leads to false forgiveness.

What appears to be anger, may really be guilt and shame. A friend of mine, a single mother, would most often get angry with her kids when they would ask her for things which were beyond her means. She felt bad because she was not able to offer a better quality of life to her children. She would lash out at them verbally when the kids would inadvertently remind her what she saw as her lack of ability as a mother. The kids would then get upset and the whole thing would escalate. Ironically what would really have helped that family's quality of life was an easy-going and happy mother not so prone to guilt.

Anger, guilt and fear can turn into a lifestyle. This could get us caught up in men/women issues, left wing/right wing, and so on. Of course it is important to deal with real world issues, but if we approach these through our unresolved personal issues our contribution is not likely to be constructive. Much of what happens in life is emotion disguised as reason. We have underlying feelings, which we express outwardly through attitudes and behaviours, and then justify these "rationally". Yet if our underlying feelings are negative and destructive there can never be a resolution. The other party will always be seen as an enemy as we will have to have a "them". While we are stuck in acting out our guilt, anger and fear we will not really want to have a resolution: we will only want to win. But when our negativity wins, everyone loses. We only truly want a win/win solution when we are committed to forgiveness and reconciliation.

Shame

Whereas guilt is a feeling of having done something bad, shame is a sense of being bad. Shame is a feeling that there is something wrong with us. If we have an underlying sense of shame it can be easily awakened when we feel guilty. We would then feel that not only was there something wrong about what we did, but also that there is something fundamentally wrong with us too.

Excess shame brings a sense of being dirty or tainted. Shame can be good in helping us moderate our behaviour to ensure that we adapt and fit in with society. It is when it goes too far that it is crippling and damaging. Shame can produce feelings of unworthiness and show itself as a false form of humility. True humility does not come from a feeling of being unworthy, or of not being good enough. True humility comes from feeling so good about ourselves that we are happy to see others do well. When we feel shame we let others shine, because we feel worthless. When we have humility we are happy to see others shine, because we feel everyone is worthy.

Many of us were even brought up to believe that it is bad to think harmful thoughts. That can make us very prone to guilt. We do not have much control of our thinking. Our thoughts seem to have a mind of their own! Believing that we are held responsible for thoughts we cannot control is like being held responsible for the thoughts of someone else.

Fear is our friend; Anger is our agent

In attempting to examine our fearful, guilty or angry reactions it is important not to treat those parts of ourselves as our enemy. Fear is our friend – sometimes at least. If it were not for fear, we would not be alive right now. Something has to stop us walking in front of a bus, or jumping out in front of a truck till we have the wisdom and experience to know why those things are not such a good idea. As we explored earlier – fear is wisdom as a child. We transform our fear into wisdom by working with it. As we grow wiser we need less fear, as we are less likely to do something really dumb.

Nature programmes us to be fearful in unfamiliar circumstances so as to keep us alive. Imagine one of our primitive ancestors walking through the jungle with a sharpened stick for a spear. He/she suddenly hears a loud rustling sound in a large bush up ahead. Which reaction is most likely to help our ancestor survive: a) "That sound could be a dangerous wild bear, I better be careful," or b) "That sound is probably a friendly fluffy bunny, I'll put my spear down and go give it a nice hug." Fear helps us moderate our behaviour till we learn a bit more of how the world works.

Anger can also work on our behalf when, like any good agent, we give it wise directions. If we are angry about being passed over for promotion, we can use that energy to take positive action; find a better job or get better at our current one. If we leave anger undirected it causes us to do things against our own long-term interest. If we become resentful and unhelpful that does not do our future prospects any good.

By taking a proactive approach to anger and having a clear intention about how we want to direct it, we become more able to get what we want without harming others. To do this we need to think about anger in a detached way. Thinking in terms of "there is anger," rather than "I am angry," can help stop us getting get caught up in those feelings. However, if we are the cool and detached type we may need to go the other way and encourage ourselves to experience our anger and let some of it out harmlessly, first.

We tend to feel anger if someone has stepped over one of our "boundaries". It helps if we can see what it is within us that is behind our reaction. If we keep our attention on them ("They should not have…" or "They should have….") this will not help us to handle the situation well. It is better to look at what was triggered in us, and in that way learn about ourselves and benefit from the experience. Did we feel hurt, or disrespected? Did they say or do something, which brings up a negative belief about ourselves? How can we heal that belief? People do what they do; it is up to us to decide whether we want to grow from it or not.

Try this:

1. Can you tell the difference between when you feel guilt or shame? If so which is the most common one for you? (Clue: guilt is how you feel about what you did, shame is how you feel about you.)

2. Think about the last time you got really angry. Was there any shame underneath it?

PART THREE

Go Deeper:
Reconcile with Yourself

Reconciliation with Ourselves

*We cannot forgive others while being
at war with ourselves.*

As we go deeper into forgiveness we also become more deeply reconciled with ourselves. There is a close connection with forgiving ourselves and being reconciled with ourselves. If we are at war with ourselves then we will find it more difficult to be forgiving towards ourselves – or anyone.

One way we get into conflict with ourselves is due to the difference between our real feelings and how we present ourselves to others. As part of fitting in with society, we learn that certain attitudes, emotions and types of behaviour meet with approval and that other attitudes, emotions and types of behaviour do not meet with approval. We learn how to fit in with the family we grow up in, we learn to fit in at the school we went to, we learn to fit in with the place we work, we learn to fit in with any groups or organizations we join. Everywhere we go, we find ourselves under pressure to fit in with stated or unstated sets of rules. This is all right up to a point, but it has side effects on how we relate to the parts of us that do not fit in. If we don't find acceptable ways to express some parts of ourselves we end up repressing them.

While growing up we are likely to experience situations where affection is not expressed outwardly, or anger is not channelled constructively or fear and uncertainty are not acknowledged or dealt with. This creates conflict within ourselves about what we want and need versus what we feel we should want and need.

The battle going on within us has to do with the difference between what we believe we should feel and how we really feel. We learn fairly early in life that it is better to tell people what they want to hear rather than what we really think or feel. In other words, we learn to not tell the truth. If we are not telling the truth, we begin to wonder if that is not the same as lying. Yet, isn't lying supposed to be bad? We are taught that it is bad to not tell the truth; yet we are also taught that it is bad (sometimes) to tell the truth. We have suffered for telling the truth; and we have also suffered for not telling the truth. No wonder we can get confused when both telling the truth and telling lies can get us into trouble!

The result of this is that we end up not telling ourselves the truth. We pretend to like people that we do not like. We pretend to trust people we do not trust, or at the very least have doubts about. We pretend to like situations that we find stressful, scary and worrying. We want to see ourselves as good and honest people. But we get pressured into hiding behind a polite mask that hides our true feelings.

We need to learn to be part of society, yet the way we learn to "fit in" creates unhealthy patterns within us. Part of the way we learn to become socialized depends on our gender. People who adopt strongly masculine roles (usually men) tend to learn to repress pain and people who adopt strongly feminine roles (usually women) tend to learn to repress anger.

The chances are that if you are man, or have a masculine role, you will be quicker to say something angers you than say it hurts you. If you are a woman, or have a feminine role, you will be more comfortable saying that something hurts you rather than saying that something angers you. However, usually hurt and anger go together. If something hurts us we usually get angry about it too. If something does not hurt, or is not harmful to us in some way, then there is not much to get angry about.

This can give us clues as to what types of things we are avoiding within ourselves. If we are mostly aware of our hurt we can begin to look at what we do with angry feelings. If we are mostly aware of our anger we can begin to look at the hurt feelings we are trying to avoid. By questioning our beliefs that anger is not acceptable, or that hurt feelings are not acceptable, we can begin to rediscover our authentic self. These parts of us are offering us a gift. There is a gift in our anger and there is a gift in our vulnerability. We need to accept these parts of us to become whole and happy people. Before we can know the truth we need to accept our truth.

We have wisely learned to hide parts of ourselves from others. This is necessary for us to survive socially. However, we do not need to hide these parts from ourselves. We can admit to ourselves how we really feel. We need to include an understanding that feelings change and grow, but we need to allow them to arise within us for that to happen.

If we explore our feelings we may discover that we have been sitting on long-term feelings of frustration, anger, fear or upset. We may find that there is someone we have to be civil towards whom we dislike or even hate. Perhaps we secretly hate our boss, or hate a colleague who we feel is after our job. Perhaps we have been pretending to like a relative of our partner, or even one of our own relatives.

On the one hand we have an instinctive response to people and situations, and on the other hand we need to behave like well-adjusted members of society.

Avoiding the issue is obviously not an answer. The internal pressure then builds up until we try to numb it by medicating ourselves using alcohol, legal and illegal drugs, excessive work, food, TV, computer games and so on. We are then blocking our instinctive responses, or deep feelings, rather than coming to terms with them. Unless we learn how to handle the parts of us that do not fit in, then we have little choice but to repress them. But they emerge anyway. They break through into our life via compulsive, addictive and unhealthy behaviour.

To reconcile with ourselves we need to allow ourselves to experience at least some of our instinctive life and re-channel it. We need to gain skill and experience in handling our instinctive nature in constructive ways. We no doubt have some skills in this already, as it is part of our development into adulthood. But the development of inner skills often gets stopped at some stage in life. We may have felt overwhelmed by what was going on within us in childhood years, in the tricky teenage years, or in the various transitions of adulthood. We might have found ourselves unable to cope with parts of our own nature and be sitting on those parts from that time.

We can explore the different themes in this section as a way of becoming reconnected and reconciled with parts of ourselves which we may have avoided or not fully acknowledged in the past. We may find that we have been denying our gifts as much as denying our wilder uncivilized parts. Some of those wilder parts may even turn out to be some of our greatest gifts.

As we explore forgiveness further we will also be exploring reconciliation with ourselves. There is a close connection with forgiving ourselves and being reconciled with ourselves. As we put an end to the war, and to the sense of struggle, within ourselves we find it easier to be forgiving towards ourselves and everyone else as well.

Try this:

1. Can you see that feeling good about yourself makes it easier to forgive others?

2. Can you see ways in which forgiving yourself would make it easier to forgive others?

The Forgiveness Garden

A garden emerges from tending the outer world;
forgiveness emerges from tending our inner world.

We do not need to understand forgiveness, and what it is, to be able to use it. This is just as well as there are some things about forgiveness that are mysterious. However, the same is true about other things in life that we manage to cope with.

My ageing mother never did understand satellite TV and how it worked so my sister showed her that pushing the buttons in a particular sequence got her what she wanted. Mum kept a note of the sequence beside the TV (first the red button, then the blue button...) and thereafter she thought satellite TV a wonderful invention as it was the only way she could get the God Channel. Forgiveness is like that: we can get away with learning what buttons to push to make it work – and we might even find ourselves tuned in to the God channel! We just need to explore a few methods, or techniques, to find the ways that work best for us.

Another analogy for forgiveness is electricity. Electricity is something we use every day, yet it is a deeply mysterious force. Even the scientists don't really understand it or know what it really is. Yet we obviously do not need to understand the fundamental nature of electricity to be able to use a toaster, switch on an electric heater, or turn up the air conditioning. Forgiveness likewise has elements of mystery about it, but we do not need to fully understand it to use it in practical and meaningful ways.

Even though aspects of forgiveness are a mystery we can understand some things about how it works. A useful analogy for forgiveness is to think of it like a garden. A garden emerges from tending our external world; forgiveness emerges from tending our inner world. We can have a specific intention to forgive, just as we can have a specific intention to create a garden, but that is just the beginning. A garden emerges from a decision and ongoing commitment; forgiveness also emerges from a similar decision and ongoing commitment. And, like a garden, forgiveness brings delights and rewards that encourage us to continue.

Planting a single tree, or a flower, on a piece of barren ground would not make that area into a garden. However, it could be the beginning of a garden. A garden emerges more and more as we plant different things. Forgiveness emerges as we develop different inner qualities. We do not need to always focus directly on forgiveness itself. By focusing on the things that allow forgiveness to emerge, we prepare the ground. Forgiveness can then emerge more easily and will sometimes spring up spontaneously.

The more we develop qualities such as acceptance, empathy, and kindness then the more readily forgiveness can emerge from within us. It is not hard to imagine that we will find it easier to forgive when we are kind and compassionate. Therefore developing such qualities makes it easier to develop a forgiving attitude.

Every gardener knows that the type of garden we can grow depends on the climate. We each have an internal climate, which depends on our typical states of thinking and feeling. The more we improve the type of thoughts we habitually focus on, and the types of feelings we cultivate, the better chance forgiveness has of taking root and flourishing. Even a very practical thing such as eating healthier food and getting sufficient exercise, can improve our state of well-being and make it easier to be forgiving; just as having healthy soil makes it easier for plants to grow.

Forgiveness does not happen in isolation. Every good thing we have learned in life helps us to learn to forgive. Every bit of wisdom we have gathered, every bit of meaning we have extracted from our experiences, every time we have grown. It all helps us to become a more forgiving person. For example, we have an experience that teaches us to have empathy for others. This in turn makes it easier to forgive as empathy helps us see things from their point of view. As we reach a deeper understanding of life, and the temptation and trials of human nature, old resentments and grudges tend to fall away.

Although we plant seeds in a garden, we don't actually make things grow and we obviously don't create the flowers. We rely on something else, in the form of the ancient and powerful forces of nature, to do its part. Likewise in forgiveness some parts of the process happen on their own. We prepare the ground, plant the seeds and, all going well, forgiveness flowers. In other words we do our part and something larger plays its part too.

This touches on the mystery of forgiveness. The mystery of forgiveness need not stop us enjoying its benefits; just as the mystery of nature does not stop us enjoying our favourite flowers. The mystery actually makes the process easier, because we only need to do part of it. There is something in nature, outside of our control, which supports the processes of growing and flowering; there is something, outside of our control, which supports the process of forgiving.

If we walk into a garden, we may notice that the feeling of "garden" emerges both from specific things, such as a flower, a tree or a bed of roses, as well as the overall experience of that place. A particular tree or a flower is something in its own right, yet it also contributes to the overall garden. The more our inner landscape is made up of empathy, kindness, compassion, the more we experience a sense of forgiveness. A garden is more than the sum of its parts; forgiveness is more than the sum of its parts too, especially as we cannot be sure when and how it will happen. We can only do our part and then await results.

Try this:

1. Imagine you feel totally loved, have everything you need, and that you really belong exactly where you are. Would this make it easier to be forgiving? Would it not mean that whatever other people said and did in the past was not so important after all?

2. Think of the feeling you get when stepping into a beautiful garden, or park (or do it for real). Notice to what extent the feelings that arise in you are about a particular thing (a flower, a tree, a bush, a border area, part of the landscape) and notice also to what extent your experience of a "garden" arises from the overall impression of that place. You may notice that the feeling of "garden" is bigger than the different parts of what makes up a garden. If forgiveness were like a garden, what for you would seem the most important things that go to make up that garden?

Forgiveness has Rhythm

Forgivingness is not an act of will;
it is an act of willingness.

It is not a matter of simply deciding to forgive and then it is done. Forgiveness is a process and the process is not completely under our conscious control. Our job is to do our part in creating the best conditions for forgiveness to occur and then to let it happen. The forgiveness process is in some ways similar to the process of falling asleep. Most of us cannot just decide to sleep and then be asleep a few seconds later.

Similarly we cannot decide to forgive and then be finished with it. Most of us have developed a rhythm or a ritual around falling asleep. We may brush our teeth, we change into our sleeping clothes, and so on. All going well, this helps get us into a state where we are more likely to fall asleep. Similarly we need rhythms and rituals around the process of forgiving to enable it to happen.

This lack of conscious control over the act of forgiveness is what sometimes prevents us from trying. If we do not know how to forgive, we are more likely to give up before we even start. We need to keep in mind that when we decide to forgive we are entering into a process. Just like other natural processes it comes about by creating the conditions that support it.

We may need to clear out anger, let go of pain and release fears and self-judgements. Anger can sometimes be released by finding a harmless physical outlet (long walks, running, hitting a cushion). The person who hurt us may not be able to hurt us again as they have died or are far away. If so we may need to remind ourselves of that till our fear diminishes. We need to make clear agreements with ourselves about what we are going to do to ensure that we will not be hurt in the same way again. We may need to talk things over with a friend or two. We may need to write a letter, in which we pour out all our feelings, which we can then burn, or otherwise destroy, to let go of all the old feelings.

If we have not forgiven then obviously something is blocking us from forgiving. Here are some of the ways we block ourselves:

- *Fear that the same thing will happen again if we forgive.*
- *Holding on to beliefs that the other person is bad or evil.*
- *Wanting revenge.*
- *Wanting justice - when the situation makes it impossible.*
- *Holding on to pain to punish ourselves "for being so stupid", and not listening to internal or external warnings.*
- *Wanting to punish ourselves for being "weak" or "vulnerable".*
- *Holding on to pain to remind ourselves to "never do that again".*
- *Believing that the more we suffer the more the other person is guilty.*
- *Feeling afraid to face the shame that we feel about our part in what happened.*
- *Wanting to prove that we were innocent as we are the hurt one.*

If we look closely we may discover that we are actually cultivating the negative feelings that keep us in an unforgiving state. The only way we can stop ourselves from forgiving is to maintain those feelings otherwise we would just forgive and move on. Unforgiveness is an active process; not a passive one.

We may not realize that we are cultivating anger, bitterness, hatred, shame or fear because we are not conscious of how we do it. It takes a lot of effort, conscious or unconscious to *not* forgive. It takes a lot of energy to stop forgiveness from happening. However, if we discover this to be true it is important not to become judgmental of ourselves because of it. In withholding forgiveness we are simply trying to protect ourselves from harm, but not realizing that the way we are going about it is causing us more harm than the original event.

They say a coward dies a thousand deaths; when we are unforgiving we hurt with a thousand pains. We experience the event time and time again in our thoughts and feelings. If we feel deep resentment towards someone, or we feel a lot of shame because of their actions, and our inability to defend ourselves at the time, we need to release self-blame before we are ready to forgive. A vital part of forgiving others is to forgive our part in what happened. We may have judgements about ourselves about having been "foolish", "weak", "stupid" or "a victim".

If we look deeper we may even discover that we hate ourselves as much as we hate our "enemy". This self-hate is really what is often behind our unwillingness to forgive. If we really like ourselves we have no interest in making ourselves unhappy. We are more likely to let go and move on. However severe or damaging the event was there is absolutely no value in keeping ourselves a prisoner of it the rest of our lives.

Forgiveness can happen even as an event is taking place. We do not need to wait till it is over. When I was staying at a hotel recently, some people were talking loudly out in the street and this was keeping me awake. I noticed that I had some heavy judgements about those people for being so loud so late at night. I began to notice how angry I was feeling and that it was partly why I was finding it hard to sleep. I was too angry to sleep. I put my attention on how my anger was keeping me awake rather than on thinking that the sound of those voices was what was keeping me awake. The next thing I knew I was waking up as it was next morning!

Previously I had noticed often it was my reaction to a particular sound that disturbed my sleep rather than the event itself. A noise may last only a few minutes, but if we get annoyed our reaction might keep us awake for hours long after the sound has gone. Similarly in more serious situations, our reaction may greatly magnify the harm done to us. An event lasting only a few minutes or a few hours may generate many years of negative emotions and greatly disturb us until we forgive.

Long held feelings of anger, rage, fear, disappointment and shame are painful. Sometimes external events can trigger those old feelings and cause us to react way beyond what is justified. If we feel pained because we feel that we were treated with disrespect in the past anything, which seems disrespectful to us, will cause those old feelings to surface. Yet the pain we experience in those situations is our creation and is not really caused by another's behaviour. Their behaviour is just a trigger for old feelings, which may have nothing at all to do with them. We may have been holding on to those feelings long before we even met them. Sometimes forgiveness is about realizing that the other person simply drew our attention to an old pain that we need to resolve.

It is important not to try and resist our reactions for this is also a form of pain. Trying to hold back our feelings is painful and exhausting. By using our awareness to disperse old painful feelings we free ourselves from their effects. This empowers us to be more in charge of how an event affects us.

We may have a strong aversion to specific feelings such as anger, hatred, self-pity and fear. We may have come to believe that such feelings are "bad" and automatically try and want to get rid of them right away. We suppress them because we do not have a socially acceptable way to express them at the time they arise. This is well and good, but then we need to ensure that we do actually deal with them later and they do not become a pool of unresolved experiences and emotions. Our ability to suppress our emotions till a more suitable time is an excellent survival strategy; yet it is not good if this becomes a habit, and if we never revisit the feeling we have suppressed.

If we have this tendency to repress or avoid some of our feelings this is something we need to forgive ourselves for. Especially since we may have caused ourselves long-term pain, just from hanging on to things and not getting round to dealing with them and resolving them. This creates a division within us where part of our inner nature is denied its place in our life. Such a split can itself be a cause of pain and confusion. Reclaiming and redeeming the neglected and rejected parts of ourselves, using our newfound skills in forgiveness, allows us to be more at peace with ourselves and more at ease in our life.

Gradually we find the middle way between the extremes of repressing feelings and being completely run by them. We allow them to be what they are, but we know that some emotions are fleeting and it would not be wise to make life-changing decisions while simply in a bad mood. We know not to leave our life partner just because we are annoyed that they keep squeezing the toothpaste tube in the middle.

Try this:

1. Think of something you need to forgive and instead of putting your attention on the other person, or the situation, put your attention on your defensive reactions. Do you notice any spiteful or vengeful, or other angry thoughts and feelings? Do you need to forgive yourself for those? If so take some time to affirm to yourself, "I forgive myself for the _____ which I feel." Example: "I forgive myself for the bitterness and hate which I feel."

2. Do you notice any self-judgements that you have towards yourself? If so try listing them and affirm to yourself, "I forgive myself and release judging myself as _____." Example: "I forgive myself and release judging myself as weak and stupid."

From Self Criticism to
Self Encouragement

If we fight with ourselves, who wins?

Nurturing and fulfilling a sense of purpose is vital to feeling good about ourselves and good about life. Sometimes in life we may suffer from a lack of a sense of purpose. When this happens we become more prone to disillusionment and doubt. A feeling of emptiness creeps in and we wonder why we bother getting up in the morning. We feel let down; let down by our own weakness, let down by those who could help us, let down by life. This can lead to a very low mix of resentment, self-recrimination, blame and bitterness.

If we feel that our life is empty we may try to find something outside ourselves to give it meaning. We might lose ourselves in frenetic activity, in making money, in running a business, in shopping, and in eating. We may also decide that such things are not enough and that only a great endeavour – such as single-handedly saving the rainforests – will justify our existence.

Meaning really comes from the inside not from the outside. When we feel that our life has no value we are really feeling that we have no value. If we base our self-worth on achieving specific goals, whether for our own benefit or for the benefit of others, we place our ability to feel good about ourselves far away from where we are now. Yet, feeling good about ourselves is what will give us the inner strength and resilience to achieve our goals in the most fulfilling way. Besides, if we leave too much of ourselves behind in striving for success there is not enough of our self left to enjoy success when we finally get there.

We may need to forgive ourselves for not being the person we aspire to be and for comparing ourselves with others rather than living the life we have. We may need to forgive life for "not being fair" and not giving us the breaks we need.

We cannot separate our life purpose from the development of our character, as they are one and the same. If we do not realize this, we can miss seeing the meaning and purpose already present in our lives. Once we understand this, that the development of our character is an essential part of our life purpose, we have a real chance of finding the deeper meaning and purpose in the ordinary events of life. The challenges and opportunities we have in life take on new meaning. We then see that all around us are exactly the right circumstances to meet our needs. In other words we are in exactly the right situation to meet our life purpose, if we can but recognize it.

Our sense of purpose can be distorted or obscured by a need for approval or wanting to be liked. If we are looking outside ourselves for validation this distances us from our purpose. Basing our thoughts and actions around other people's opinions of us only works if their opinion is in line with the next step in our progress. If someone has spent much of their life as Marshmallow Man, just agreeing with everyone and not standing up for himself, some of the people around him are not going to like it when he finally wakes up and learns to assert himself. Yet, there is no way that such a person can express much of a sense of purpose until they have gone through such an awakening. Their character needs to change as part of the process of discovering their purpose.

Being at the mercy of the whims and opinions of others is not going to help us feel good about ourselves for very long. If life feels empty then maybe it is indeed empty. It is empty of us, if we are not present. We are not present when we live life too much in need of another's approval. Ultimately it is our own approval that we need and we can only have that by living by our own values. Connecting with what is truly important to the best that is within us, and exploring how to express it, is what makes life feel full and rich.

It can be lovely to have the approval of other people. As long as the approval is not at the expense of an important value that we hold, it can be very healthy. It is only if we start sacrificing important parts of ourselves to another's approval that it becomes a problem. If we give up an important inner calling, just because someone will not like it we become unbalanced. A friend of mine loved playing guitar in a local band. His new wife announced that she "hated" the sound of electric guitar – so he gave it up! Their relationship did not last. Another friend was the other guitarist in the same band. His wife loved to hear him play and encouraged him. Their relationship lasted. These are the kinds of choices we can make to help connect with the deeper parts of ourselves.

- *The choice to be kind to someone we don't really like.*
- *The choice to overcome our irritation with a person who really annoys us.*
- *The choice to face our fear of confronting or negotiating with someone in authority.*

- *The choice to stand by a friend in need, or to take a stand on principle.*
- *The choice to leave a situation, which has become chronically unhealthy.*
- *The choice to practise forgiveness on an active and regular basis.*

If we feel the need to find a worthy life purpose all we need to do is look around us. What is most missing in the world? What does the world need more of? How about forgiveness? Why not make this the focus of our life purpose? We could also choose some other worthy quality to develop such as compassion, empathy, kindness or love. Meeting the challenges of living up to such a purpose does not depend on us making a grand outer gesture, or winning X Factor, it depends on how we respond to the small things happening in daily life.

A simple event can be given an incredible depth of meaning simply by how we respond to it. Something may happen which irritates us. We could just leave it at that, so that the event just "means" that we got irritated. We could also choose to give it a much deeper meaning by making that event a step towards forgiveness and feelings of connection and compassion. It can mean we look beyond superficial human behaviour and look at the causes of that behaviour within others and ourselves. As we release our judgements and are able to see the causes of our own behaviour we also begin to see the causes of events in the world around us. We connect with a deeper understanding and a deeper wisdom. We also connect with the goodness and beauty of life. Not a bad outcome to get out of one annoying person! (Maybe we should pay them to stick around.)

Rather than trying to find our purpose, perhaps our purpose is finding us. It is finding us in the ordinary events of every day, and looking for us to give our best. If we try and transfer materialistic ambitions into ambition for inner achievement then we just get a muddy mix and a cause of frustration. We end up being ambitious to do more good than others, to be better at saving the planet than others, and we may even become ambitious to be better than anybody else at being humble.

Try this:

1. Do you feel that you need to achieve certain goals in order to be worthy as a person? What if you are okay just as you are? Could you still achieve those goals but in a more enjoyable and relaxed way?

2. Do you tend to value other people mostly in terms of how they help you achieve your goals? How would it be to enjoy people for their own sake?

Watching What
We Broadcast

*To change our life we need to
change what we broadcast.*

I have a friend who is extremely sensitive and I have learned not to make some types of joking comments around her. She gets offended even when I say things that most people would laugh at. It is not only me who affects her this way and she admits to being "a bit sensitive". When she is hurt by such comments, who causes her hurt? Is it herself, is it me, or is it both of us?

In our wiser moments, we all know that it is our interpretations of events which cause our hurt feelings, rather than the event itself. If we said "Hello" to a friend and they ignore us, we would most likely feel offended. If we found out later they had just received really bad news and were in shock, we would switch from feeling offended to feeling a wave of sympathy. The outer specifics are still the same; all that changed was our interpretation. When we interpret an event differently the feelings we have around it change too. How do we know that we are interpreting an event accurately? We do not know unless we ask the other person what was going on with them.

Whether something offends us or not depends on how we feel at the time. If we are feeling particularly insecure, fearful or angry we are more likely to be easily offended. If we are bothered by what someone says to us at such times, is forgiveness really the issue? What was really bothering us was our own inner state. Blaming someone else for that (and then believing that they need our forgiveness) is inappropriate. If someone hits a raw nerve, we can choose to rise above it and realize that we are just a bit touchy at the moment. If we are not able to do that then we are blaming people for things that are really our own creation.

Our interpretation of events shapes our attitude to life. Our attitude then becomes self-fulfilling and self-sustaining, as our attitude is something that we cannot help transmit to others. It has been said that only 7% of communication is words. The rest is body language, tone of voice and so on. A person's body language can unconsciously trigger how we respond to them without us being aware of it. If we become aware of those triggers we can look beyond superficial interactions and see what is going on underneath.

We constantly broadcast our attitude to all around us. We send messages such as, "I'm a victim," "Don't mess with me," or "Please don't hurt me," depending on our inner state. Other people react to our messages either positively or negatively and it affects the types of people and experiences we attract. When we ask ourselves, "Why is this happening to me?" the answer may lie in what we "broadcast" through our body language and tone of voice.

Moreover, what we do not say can broadcast louder than what we say. If we never express appreciation to our friends, then they are not likely to feel appreciated by us. If we rarely go out of our way to be friendly, then others may feel that we are not their friend. As the old saying goes: "If you want a friend, be a friend."

We can usually tell whether we are dealing with a happy, easygoing person or an uptight neurotic one. We may not be aware of how we know this, but we usually get a sense of what a person is like. Likewise, people react to our unspoken feelings such as anger, fear or guilt, which we communicate through our behaviour.

• • • • •

I recently overheard a guy at a party proclaim that he is happy to be just a friend to a very attractive woman that he knows. His words said that he was okay with it, but the whine in his voice said he was not happy about it at all. His tone of voice really said, "Why does this keep happening to me!" He seemed to have no idea how much of how he really felt was being broadcast to anyone who bothered to look beyond his words. His denial of his true feelings did not stop them being obvious.

We have all seen situations where someone was broadcasting anger or hostility, but were putting on a smiley face. The person was on the defensive – which is a form of pre-emptive counter-attack. Sometimes the person doing this may be reacting out of fear or anger. They were expecting a difficult situation and their attitude helped make it that way. It is not hard to see why such a stance can easily become self-fulfilling if others start to react to that person's unconscious aggression.

Of course, other people cannot sense everything that is going on inside us. Besides, if necessary, people will often give us the benefit of the doubt. However, some of the things, which come our way, have to do with what we are broadcasting – even though we are not aware of it.

If we notice inexplicable events happening to us: people avoiding us for no apparent reason, getting unexpected reactions from others, then it is good to look at what we are transmitting. However, we need to forgive ourselves if we have been attracting unhappy experiences because of our unconscious communications, through tone of voice and general demeanour.

Try this:

1. Record a soap opera off the TV and play it back with the sound off. See how much you can tell about what is going on by the body language of the actors. If there is a fight or an argument, notice how the people spark each other as things escalate. Play it again at a crucial point and put words on the stance or body language of the different characters. Is it: "Don't mess with me," "Don't hurt me," "I'm going to get you," or what? If the actors are good this should not be too difficult. Otherwise try another soap opera. Is your body language ever like any of those characters?

2. Imagine a situation where you feel challenged. Get in to the physical stance you would normally have for that situation. What do you broadcast? What tone of voice do you use? Are you aware of any timidity or aggression you are putting out? Try and not judge yourself, but instead feel empathy, compassion and kindness for your character in that situation.

Death is Character Forming

Resisting pain causes more pain.

Pain, suffering, disease and death are parts of life that we usually want to avoid. We wonder why they exist and wish we could get rid of them. Depending on our beliefs, we need to forgive life, God, or Fate for the existence of such horrors. Yet, pain, suffering, disease and death cannot be wished away and how we handle them shapes our character.

If we find ourselves facing physically painful conditions we may wonder why this is happening to us. If the pain is caused by a life-threatening disease some give up and surrender to death; others fight on as long as they can. Which is the better option, to fight or to surrender? When we see someone faced with a lot of pain, yet fighting to stay alive, we may wonder why they do so. We may question, why don't they just give up and let death happen? After all death can't be as bad as what they are experiencing, can it? It may seem an easy choice to us as an onlooker, but that is partly because we are not the one facing death.

Fighting to stay alive despite being in pain, is probably only partly due to the fear of death. The fear of pain (or fear of more pain) will also be present and this will partly cancel out the fear of death. Much of our life experience teaches us when to resist and when to surrender. This is one of the core polarities which life offers us: when to give up and when to carry on. If we want to strengthen ourselves, and be more self-determining, then resisting the process of disease and dying could (up to a point) be a very good way to do that.

Some who have recovered from a serious accident, where they were close to death, have commented that the hard part was deciding to stay alive and facing the pain of recovery; the easier option would have been to surrender to the peace and ease of death. They chose the harder option as they felt that they had more work to do here on the earth.

In doing so they are developing important qualities; qualities of courage, resilience and strength. The urge to grow and develop runs deep and even in the face of death some of us will not give up and will look for ways to enhance our character even through that experience. Our character develops from birth to death no matter what is happening to the body. How we respond to pain and to life-threatening disease is both an expression of our character and part of the development of our character.

We most rapidly develop our character in situations that involve intensity and focus. Few things create intensity and focus as effectively as the imminent possibility of death. Therefore, it could be said that death is character building! If we do not believe in an afterlife or reincarnation, and we are facing death, then we may not see much point in any form of personal development. However, even then we might still feel a curious compulsion to take it as a challenge.

Facing death challenges us in numerous ways all at the same time. At each stage we are faced with important and unavoidable decisions. Each decision we make could result in a full recovery or in an early demise. Do we use mainstream medicine, holistic medicine or both? Do we change our diet, lifestyle, or our work? Do we work on finding emotional or psychological causes? The possible consequences of making the "wrong" choice force us to deepen our sense of connection with ourselves and with our deepest beliefs.

In order to make the best choices we have to make decisions based on the *knowing* of the deepest and wisest parts of ourselves. In this way we develop skills of intuition and of inner connection. We develop great resilience, courage and endurance. We develop qualities in ways that may not have happened, or only have happened very slowly, if we had not been faced with such challenging circumstances.

On the one hand we can look at a person with a painful life-threatening condition superficially and see them as someone who is apparently trying to stay alive out of an understandable fear of death. Alternatively we can look deeper and see the ways in which the person is growing from within themselves. All non-essential parts of themselves are falling away and they are connecting with what is most important.

We can see that even in the face of death – the supposed end to this life – something is being born. There is something within the human spirit calling a person to continue with their growth and to continue with their development. In this way even death itself becomes a life-enhancing experience.

What can trigger us to delve deeper into our capacities and abilities may not be something life threatening. This can also happen if we are severely challenged by something impacting on our sense of self. A challenging job or challenging relationship can do that too. A friend who found himself in a very tough job told me, "I don't mind it being tough for now. I am actually enjoying the challenge. When I've had enough, then I'll quit." He was willing to accept the challenge because he could see it was helping develop parts of his character.

Just as my friend needed to think beyond his current job, perhaps we need to see the bigger picture and see the development of our character as being something bigger than the life we have now. Our present life is just for a short span, but our character is timeless.

Try this:

- Does the inevitability of death distort how you live your life?
- Can you forgive the fact that your current life is not permanent?

The Gift in the Wound

Every wound offers us a gift.

It is easier to forgive situations where we felt wounded if we can see the gift in the wound. Seeing the gift in the wound means seeing what was good about a situation even if it means we need to stretch our imagination to find anything. This does not mean we need deny the difficulties and the challenges. On the contrary, we need to fully accept difficulties and challenges to gain the gifts that those situations offer us.

Looking for the gift in the wound helps us be more philosophical and detached about events. It helps us look beyond the superficial and see how we can grow from our experiences. If we are honest with ourselves, about the ways in which we feel challenged, we are more likely to be able to face those challenges and draw benefits from them. We learn how to extract something deeper and more profound out of life events. We extract healing where before we only experienced pain. We extract insights where before we only experienced confusion. We extract meaning where before, the event or situation seemed pointless.

We have a capacity to turn every experience to the good. Whether the cause was misunderstanding, deliberate attempt to harm us, or someone angrily trying to defend themselves from real or imagined hurts. The motive of the other person is irrelevant, as it has nothing to do with our ability to make something good out of a situation. Even the willingness to try and find goodness in our difficulties makes a difference and lifts us out of the mud. The attempt to look deeper takes us beyond ourselves and calls upon parts of us that are deeper and wiser than our normal day-to-day selves.

Say for example, from childhood onwards we have experiences of being disappointed and let down by people. We can either become bitter and withdrawn, or we can learn to be self-reliant and know what we need to do to take care of ourselves. We can also use the experience to learn to be more sensitive to the needs of others in similar situations. Are there ways in which we may be hurting others without realizing it? In this way the wound of, "feeling let down by others" can become the gifts of "greater self-reliance", or "greater sensitivity to others".

Or we may feel a lack of connection with others – perhaps we became too self-reliant. We can turn this wound of "lack of connection" into the gift of "learning to trust" by learning all about trust; how to trust, who to trust and when to trust. Most of us have had experience of finding the gift in the wound without realizing it. As we recognize this ability it gets stronger. Our capacity to find the gift grows when we allow ourselves to acknowledge and nurture it.

By looking for the gift in the wound we lift our mind above the victim stance of "Why did this happen to me?" and "What did I do to deserve this?" Instead our questions become, "How can I make something good out of this?" and "What can I get from this which will make me happier?" Granted we may sometimes need to dig deeply to come up with something. Nevertheless this kind of thinking will help get us into a more empowered frame of mind. When we are able to handle the things which hurt us, then we are much more able to handle any other part of life.

Sometimes the gift in the wound is simply a lesson about staying away from certain types of people and certain types of situations. Sometimes it is in learning to live with our own temporary limitations. Sometimes the gift is a lesson in learning to listen to our inner warning system when it says, "Don't go there," or "Don't do that!" At other times the gift may be a profound insight into an aspect of life that previously baffled or confused us. As we develop our willingness and ability to see the gifts life offers us we go beyond ourselves and our current limitations. New potentials and capacities begin to awaken within us and then we see ourselves differently and we see life differently. We transform previously hurtful experiences into ones of liberation and empowerment.

I have had people sometimes point out to me that I "might just possibly be a bit autistic" because of how I relate to the world. I sometimes tend to pause and not say anything when others might respond. This "wound" has caused me problems in some social situations, but has been a real gift in other ways. It has allowed time for me to find another way to respond to situations rather than re-acting in a way which would escalate them. It has helped me move from a reactive response to life to a creative one.

It has often saved me from threatening situations as my reaction (which is sometimes no reaction) is so unusual that it baffles the perpetrators. I am trying to figure out whether I am afraid of someone, and they mistake my apparent lack of fear as extreme confidence and wonder what is behind it and become wary. By the time I realize, "Oh, I am afraid," I have already managed to blurt out something that defused the situation.

· · · · ·

Gang members in areas of Glasgow sometimes go to the young men in other areas and challenge them by saying, "We are from (whichever part of Glasgow they are from) and we rule this place!" I once lived in an area just outside Glasgow called East Kilbride and was waiting at a bus stop when a guy came out of a wandering group of young men and snarled at me, "We are from Cambuslang and we rule this place!" I answered him in a similar tone, "Then you are welcome to it!" as if I were disgusted with the place. Whatever reactions he was expecting, that was not among them. He turned away a bit and leaned back against a railing, folding his arms and looking despondent as if someone had taken away a favourite toy.

He reminded me of those episodes in Star Trek where Captain Kirk would confuse a robot by giving a response it did not expect and the robot would shut down. He was a bit drunk and surly so I kept a discrete eye on him (and an alert but non-threatening stance) till he wandered off to rejoin his friends. I did not miss him when he left.

Another time I was waiting at a bus stop in a rough area of London at about 3am. A gang of youths appeared, spread right across the street, and headed in my direction. Suddenly one of them broke away from the others and started running straight towards me. I did not know what to do so I just watched him. He was getting closer and closer. My youthful interest in Karate had dwindled away long before and I had no illusions about being some kind of martial art hero, so I kept a neutral stance and just watched him. When he got close he suddenly stopped, shouted "Boo!" turned round and ran back to his friends. They all gave me a wide berth as they went past. Outwardly I stayed neutral and watched them go. I was very glad when the bus finally came.

If my feisty personality had been fully engaged during those two events I could have got myself into big trouble. However, as I tend to somehow freeze at crucial times a wiser part of me could intervene, or could at least keep me neutral, and things worked out a lot better. In this way my wound (which some call "being on the autistic spectrum") has given me a precious gift and may well have saved my life.

Try this:

1. Think of a situation which you found challenging (in the beginning it is better not to use one which is highly charged emotionally). Ask yourself, "What benefits did I get from that situation?" "What benefits could I have got from that situation?" and "Is there a gift in the wound?" Write a list of

gifts on a piece of paper. Try to not judge or filter your answers and just let them flow.

2. Imagine you are travelling along a path that goes up a mountain. You come to a cave that is known as The Cave of The Wise One. You sit outside this cave and eventually The Wise One comes out and sits in front of you. Tell The Wise One about a situation which you do not understand and ask what you can learn or how you can benefit from that situation. Wait for the answer. When he/she has finished, imagine yourself thanking her/him then returning back down the mountain. Open your eyes and write what you learned.

Getting Needs Met

To get what we need, we need to forgive.

Forgiveness is a very good way to get what we want in life. This may seem surprising till we look deeper and see the ways in which we hold ourselves back from getting what we want. Forgiveness can help us overcome feelings of being undeserving, owing to guilt or shame. It can help us heal wounds from the past where our needs were denied.

Those wounds may be keeping us from having the inner strength or courage to take the steps we need to take to have our needs met, in the present. If we feel emotionally damaged, and we do not forgive those we see as the cause, we can end up behaving in ways that keep us damaged as we feel unable to rise above the situation.

If we are rejected and feel bitter or angry then we behave in ways that make it harder to get our needs met. We become afraid to take chances, afraid to reach out, and afraid to connect with others in meaningful ways. We can even end up trying to get what we want in unhealthy, manipulative or devious ways. Forgiveness frees us from the past and enables us to get what we want in healthy ways.

If we build our life around coping with painful feelings of disappointment or rejection we limit what we can achieve. We are focused on not getting hurt rather than being focused on getting what we want. Of course we want to avoid being hurt, but to focus on a negative is like trying to drive a car by only looking in the rear-view mirror. Rather than looking at something behind us and saying, "I don't want to go there," it's better to look forward and say, "I want to go there."

One of the times that the opportunity to forgive arises is when we are denied something we need. If we can find other ways to meet that need it becomes much easier to forgive the person who denied us. Unmet needs can become locked up inside us, particularly if we experienced abuse and were treated aggressively.

Accepting that we have needs, and that they are a normal part of life, helps us stop blaming ourselves for not being invulnerable and, crucially, stop giving ourselves a hard time because we need other people. As we release guilt and shame about having our needs met we become more reconciled with ourselves and more able to forgive ourselves and others. We learn to let go of the old hurts and shame-filled thoughts about "neediness" and find healthy ways to take care of ourselves.

A forgiving attitude puts us in a more positive frame of mind to go after what we want and increases our chances of success. If we spend too long smarting with resentment because someone let us down, or something did not turn out how we planned, we can be missing the opportunities right in front of us. If we do not forgive we may become too bitter or too afraid to take a chance. In a negative frame of mind we can convince ourselves that things never work in our favour so it's not worth trying.

This is a self-fulfilling prophecy because if we are not willing to try then nothing is going to happen. Most people who are successful experienced many failures along the way, but they just did not give up.

In relationships we are more likely to get more of what we want by forgiving than by resenting. If someone does not, or cannot, give us what we want we forgive them and move on. This stops us wasting our time and energy. Forgiveness frees us from situations, which are not going to work in our favour. If we want a committed relationship and the other person only wants a casual relationship, rather than resisting and struggling we can just forgive and let go. We will find someone else more suitable, more quickly, that way.

Getting entangled, via unforgiveness, with those who cannot meet our needs is a waste of time and is not necessary. When we get entangled with those who cannot meet our needs it is like being caught in a net and being stuck somewhere we do not want to be. The answer is to escape from the net, as more struggling just gets us more in a tangle. Forgiveness is what allows us to escape the net. We then have a chance to meet people who are a better match.

If we are upset by a situation it is often because we are getting the opposite of what we want. We want respect and we get disrespect, we want affection and we get treated coldly. We begin to associate some of our needs with a sense of lack, or with painful thoughts and feelings. We may tend to avoid those needs as it is painful to go near them. We may feel numbness or pained when these needs come up again later. We struggle with ourselves, as the need keeps coming up and we keep pushing it away. However, if we do not accept our needs we cannot expect anyone else to accept them either.

Such needs have obviously not gone away. If we can unpack our needs from any distressing or painful associations we have around them, we can find ways to meet them. We can look for ways to meet our needs in the present and not expect someone else to change or be caught up in the impossibility of changing the past. A couple may fight because one of them does not want to visit the other's parents. Instead of fighting about it they can find other meaningful things to do together.

We may feel disappointed because our boss does not like some of our ideas – the ones that we think are particularly good. Rather then feeling offended we can put our energy into finding other ideas which our boss will really like – or into finding another job where we will be really appreciated. We can get what we want more often when we are not too insistent about how it comes about.

If someone hurts us it is best to be careful that we do not get fixated on that person and unconsciously expect resolution or healing to come from him or her. Wishing that people would change to suit our needs is not a winning strategy – especially if the person is dead and gone. We may keep coming back to the same core issues such as, "My father did not love me," "My boss does not treat me with respect," or "My husband never listens to me." Too much of that type of thinking can put us into a stupor. We need to interrupt that type of thinking with a good strong, "So what!" and instead look at the underlying need so that we can find other ways to get it met.

It is important that we take ownership of our needs rather than assuming that someone else "should" meet them, or assuming that an important need will always remain unmet. We can learn to run with our needs rather than being run by them. We have the need to be loved, the need to be respected, the need to be heard. It could even be argued that we have the right to such things, but this is not served by expecting too much from any specific person who is just not able or willing to respond.

Instead we accept that these are healthy and valid needs and can take action from a position of ownership to do something about them. Usually this means broadening our circle so that we have more options for getting what we want.

There is a saying in dating circles that if someone gets rejected they should, "Go date ten other people." The reason this works is that it takes their mind off moping around and obsessing about one particular person. It gives them a meaningful and related challenge to think about instead. The same principle applies where other important needs are not being fulfilled: go meet ten other people.

Maybe we are right and our father or mother did not love us. We can decide it was just how they were and move on. It does not say anything about us if someone does not love us. They were just not capable of it and that is all there is to it. If our boss does not respect us we can decide that it is his problem and can look around to where we can get respect. If our partner does not listen to us we can decide that he/she is just not a great listener and get that need met somewhere else. Relying too much on specific people to meet specific needs, when they can't or won't, just creates suffering.

The Power of "AND"

There is no point in wanting someone to love us who is not much capable of loving anyone. We may still be yearning for something from someone who is long dead or long gone. We may have needs locked up in the past where we cannot do anything about them. The answer is to bring such needs into present time and to ask ourselves, "What do I need NOW to be happy?"

One way we can prevent ourselves from focusing on self-defeating thoughts is by adding the word "and" to extend the phrase which describes the issue, e.g., "My father did not love me, AND I can get lots of love from other people." "The person I want as a life partner just wants to be friends, AND I am looking for someone even better." "My finances are a mess, AND I have a meeting next week to get that sorted."

We may be carrying our angst around with us to show it to our friends – like it was something we bought in a sale. Our underlying message becomes, "Look how awful my life is...," or "Listen to how terrible my partner is...." If too much of our conversation is like that then it is time to find a healthier role in life. We may enjoy showing other people that our personal drama is as bad, or worse, than theirs. However we will soon tire of this, or if we don't, our friends probably will. It is far better to look at solving our underlying issues, and make peace with life.

We can build our sense of self around successfully meeting our needs rather than the comic-tragic ways in which they are not met. Looking to how we can find love and nurturing in the present can help us avoid old pitfalls and heal old hurts. Abuse from parents, or other carers, is particularly hurtful partly because they ought to be a source of love and nurturing.

Yet we have to look to the present rather than to the past to resolve those needs. Being focused on the hurt attached to a need is not the same as focusing on the need. If we are focused on the hurt it is like holding our finger on the repeat button and we keep repeating the same bad experiences.

A champion mountain biker noted for winning competitions in very dangerous terrain was asked why he was so successful. He said, "I put my attention on where I want to go; not on where I don't want to go." He kept his attention on the path in front no matter how rough, muddy or bumpy it got. He did not put his attention on the big drop just to the side of a narrow path he was on – as he did not want to go there.

Where many of us really want to "go" is to have the experience of love on a regular basis. This is one of our deepest needs and can cause us to obsess about ways in which love has been, or is being denied us. This causes us to see love as something we need to get; when it is really something we need to give. When we give it we will get plenty back.

What wounded us the most were the people unable to love us properly because they were locked into their own fear and pain. If we are not able to love others properly because we also are locked into our own fear and pain then we are perpetuating the problem.

Forgiveness frees us from false issues to focus on the real one. We do not suffer from psychological "complexes" but from a "simplex": the need to give and receive love. Forgiveness enables us to tap into our capacity to love and be loved. The people we respond to in unloving ways are usually wounded and lack skill in getting their needs met. Yet those may very well be the people who need our love the most. This does not mean that we need to put up with abusive behaviour. Not everyone can accept our love no matter how much they need it, but there are plenty of others who will accept us being as loving as we want.

Can we ever be truly happy until we give our best? Why wait for someone perfectly lovable to come along before we give the world the best we have to offer? That kind of waiting does not work. Rather than waiting for that perfect person, we need to fill our life with love for the people around us.

Nothing is more attractive than a person in love with life. Nothing is more likely to attract the perfect partner, or the perfect job, than someone putting as much love as they can into the life they already have.

We get our deepest needs met by learning to forgive so that we are free to love.

Try this:

1. Are there needs you have which you try and avoid having? Are there needs you have which you feel guilty and ashamed about? Have you ever felt that an important need was rejected, or caused you to be rejected?

Give the need a name and say to yourself a number of times, "I forgive myself for needing [name the need]." Then ask yourself, "How can I now meet my need for [name the need] in healthy ways?" Notice any answers that come to you over the next few days.

2. Who or what do you need to forgive so that you can love more?

Have Your Parents
Forgiven You?

*What we think are issues we have with our parents
are really issues we have with life.*

Have your parents forgiven you? The idea that we need to forgive our parents has become somewhat of a cliché. What is often overlooked is our parents may have plenty reasons for needing to forgive us.

Being willing to look at our issues with our parents' from another perspective, especially from the other side (i.e. from our parents' perspective) can be invaluable. It can give us a sense of empathy and connection with them. It brings a deeper understanding of them beyond the roles we play in each other's lives. This helps us be less judgmental and more forgiving.

Forgiving our parents is easier if we have some understanding of their experience in raising us and of the challenges this created for them. Have you ever watched a parent having to battle with a child going through the "terrible twos" and the various temper tantrums? Did you notice how hard that can be on a parent? Did we not also behave like that at one time? Probably. Of course we were just innocent children, but it might not always have seemed that way to our parents. Have you never seen a child appear to be wilfully destructive or disobedient? Perhaps we sometimes behaved like that too. I suspect I probably did. Then of course there are the various challenges we put them through as we got older. Resisting starting school, resisting doing homework, resisting doing housework, fighting with our siblings, and so on.

A friend of mine, who was a single mum, would go through regular bouts of parental guilt after getting angry with her three kids for squabbling so much. To make her laugh I made up a saying (delivered in an overly-earnest, preachy voice): "Home is about creating a cosy, safe and loving place where children can fight with each other."

Were our parents such perfect creatures that they never felt even a hint of resentment towards us because of our behaviour? We are usually quick enough to judge them as imperfect as we get older. Yet, at the same time, we still assume they are so perfect as to never have resented us throughout our whole childhood.

Parents are not "allowed" by society to resent their children. Perhaps their reactions all build up and boil over sometimes and that explains some of their actions if they were unkind towards us. They may lash out at us and then feel guilty about it later. They may have no idea how to resolve their guilt feelings as they have amassed so many of them from all the "mistakes" that they made. They may need to forgive themselves.

Later as adults we may start telling our parents how they ought to improve their lives. We may spout the latest self-help theory we have come across and be surprised that they are not exactly bowled over by the great ideas we are offering them. They can remember when we dribbled and drooled our way through the day and when even eating a cracker, without getting most of it down our front, was a major triumph. They helped us through the stage when we had no control over our basic biological functions, so they may wonder why we think we have the right to give them advice. They can probably remember when we would whine childishly about this or that and to them our "helpful advice" may sound like more of the same.

Life Issues

Some of the issues we think we have with our parents have nothing to do with them. Many of our issues are life issues and are not about the specific people we had as parents. We would have had those issues with any parents no matter what they were like. We may have issues about life and its meaning, issues about the state of the world, issues about our purpose in the world and so on. It is not our parents' fault if we have these issues, such things are just part of life.

Our parents were probably a couple of relatively inexperienced people who raised us by stumbling along the best they knew how. What they knew about raising kids they probably got from their own parents, who probably stumbled along too. We cannot resolve deep life issues through them, as they are just ordinary people.

We may think our parents brought us into the world. But think again. It was the process of life that brought us here. Our parents are not responsible for us being born, because they did not even know us. Yes, they helped bring somebody into the world, but they did not know who it was till we showed up! We did not even have a name, so they had to make something up. It's not like they got a chance to interview us first to find out if we are compatible with them! We just turned up expecting them to look after us. Our parents simply played a part in something much bigger than themselves – which is what we all do.

Forgiving our parents is about accepting who they are *not* as much as accepting who they are. Our parents may have been very smart, astute, and capable people, or they may have not been. What did they know? Maybe not a lot. Whose fault is that? Maybe not really anyone's. We may feel that they should have known better. Why? We have much better psychological and self-help tools at our disposal than they ever had, yet we still struggle with getting our act together. What chance did they have?

Every child has certain characteristics that show themselves early on. Some are shy, some are outgoing, some laugh a lot and some don't. This partly depends on the environment, but it also depends on the child's character. What we see as childhood problems can be the first appearance of lifelong themes in the development of our character. We are not just shaped by our childhood; our childhood was also shaped by us. The issues we face in life are present in our childhood because our childhood is also part of our life.

We may spend our whole life developing and growing and learning to handle the challenges of life. Our childhood is simply the start of the process. Our parents are obvious candidates for blame, as the first people with whom we experience some of our core life issues, but that does not mean they caused those issues. Their behaviour may have triggered the issues and raised our awareness of them, but that does not necessarily mean that it is their fault that we have such issues. It could be those are simply our set of issues, which are our focus for learning in this life.

I was sometimes a tempestuous child and now I am sometimes a tempestuous adult. This is a character issue I have: how to stay calm and not get angry and upset about things. I faced that issue as a child and I face it as an adult too. My parents were sometimes very skilled in how they handled me, but I seem to more easily remember the times they were not. It seems superficially appealing to blame my parents for my character issues and believe that if all my development needs had been met as a child then I would be better adjusted to handle the world. But did any one ever have all their childhood development needs met? Isn't it better to experience real people as parents to prepare us for the way the world really is now?

We might wonder what fine and well-adjusted people we would be if only we had received more love and attention as children. Maybe not. I have a friend who as a child was doted on not only by his parents but also by three adoring sisters. His life is a mess. He expects things to just fall in his lap and has no energy to make things happen. He got what many of us feel that we missed, but if we see the effects of the alternative we could decide that our childhood was not so bad after all.

If we have a character issue around feeling unloved, it is likely to show up first with our parents. Anything they do which looks like it means that we are unloved will trigger the issue – even though another child might have responded very differently to exactly the same experience. If later in life other people's behaviour trigger the same issue it is because that's a character issue we are working on.

All parents make mistakes, get overwhelmed, get irritated and lose their temper with their kids. How we interpreted their actions and how we responded was a choice. As kids we may not have had the experience to make great choices, and our options may have been very limited, but they are still choices. We learn more by noticing the effects of our choices than by blaming our parents or by blaming ourselves.

We may have been unfortunate enough to have cruel and stupid parents. That can be a tough one. Maybe it helps to accept that is just how they were. *"Oh my parents were cruel and stupid, that's why they were mean. It was nothing much to do with me after all."* By removing some of the sting and by realizing it was nothing personal we can get on with our lives more readily. Most of us had parents who were not particularly good or particularly bad. But it boils down to: *"It was nothing much to do with me after all."*

Some say we choose our parents. Whether it is by choice, by fate, or by accident we still end up with parents from the available stock. The available stock of human beings, which includes us, has a bit further to go before reaching perfection. Our parents may have screwed up big time simply because they are part of the current level of evolution of the human race – and all its fault and foibles. There is no point in taking our parents' imperfections personally.

There may be specific issues and specific incidents with our parents that we want to work on forgiving. But we need to free ourselves from wanting our parents to change. Life cannot be different without us becoming different. Wanting our parents to change keeps us dependent. It means our happiness depends on them, and we are stuck in our childhood.

To claim the benefits of our childhood we need to see our childhood experiences as a source of insight and wisdom rather than as a source of pain. By examining how we responded as a child and how we respond now we can build a bridge in our awareness between our childhood and the present. Throughout life we make choices then face the consequences of those choices. The consequences we experience help us to make different, or better, choices in the future.

The more we can honour this natural process of choices and consequences, and leave aside the tendency to blame either our parents or ourselves, the more readily we can learn from our choices.

Try this:

1. If either of your parents are still around, and you get on reasonably well together, ask them what was the hardest thing about raising you. Ask them what made you challenging to bring up. See if you can listen without getting annoyed.

2. If your childhood was truly awful you may be tempted to ask, "Why did this happen to me?" Instead try asking yourself a number of times, "How do I forgive my parents and move on with my life?" and notice what answers come up in the days ahead.

3. Ask your parents, "When raising me what do you wish you had done differently?"

De-cluttering Our Emotions

Letting go of pain and forgiveness are the same thing.

It is easy to tell if we have really forgiven. Does thinking about the person or event still make us upset or angry? If so, then we have not forgiven and have a bit of work to do if we want to be free of that piece of our past. There may be old feelings to let go of if they are having an unhealthy and unproductive effect on how we live now.

It is obviously harder to forgive something if it has caused us a lot of pain. However, it is also true that it is easier to forgive if we don't feel much pain. This gives us a clue as to how to make it easier to forgive. If we can reduce the pain – by releasing it and letting it go – we find it easer to forgive. If are still holding onto the pain then it is much harder to forgive. If the pain or anger from an event feels like a vague distant memory then there is not much stopping us from forgiving. If the pain or anger feels very intense then it is going to be harder to forgive as the pain is still fresh – even if the event itself was a long time ago. In releasing the painful effects we find it easier to forgive the cause.

When an old painful memory comes up, especially one where we feel a lot of charged emotions, it can be good to ask ourselves how long ago the event happened. We may be surprised to discover heated emotions from things which happened many years ago, or even many decades ago. It is then good to ask ourselves "How long ago did this happen?" "Do I want to sacrifice my present happiness to this?" and "How much longer do I want to keep this old issue going on inside me?

We may be temped to think that the other person does not deserve to be forgiven but this is forgetting that we really forgive to benefit ourselves as much as anything else. Forgiveness frees us from at least some of the consequences of their actions, but it does not free them from the consequences of their action. Forgiveness may even free us from all the consequences of their action because if we no longer feel wounded we become more socially mobile and can do a better job of getting what we want in the different spheres of life.

If someone stole from us we may carry a wound around the issue of trusting others. Because of this we may miss out on some wonderful opportunities owing to our refusal to take any risks because of our fear and lack of forgiveness. Once we forgive we can take a more balanced view and can better judge what opportunities are worth taking a risk. There are few things we can benefit from which do not involve some degree of risk so it is a matter of being able to judge the risk and not have a knee-jerk response of avoiding all risks.

We may find that we want to hold on to a painful situation. We may be holding on to a painful experience to remind ourselves "not to make the same mistake again." That can be a form of self-punishment for being "fooled" or "taken in" by someone. This is a bizarre logic as the amount of pain we are causing ourselves is many times more than the original event itself, and it is also many times more than what we would experience even if we did actually repeat the same mistake.

Letting Go

We can all find our own favourite ways of letting go of old emotions. Letting go usually needs to include some form of expression of the anger and hurt – sometimes a lot of expression! Practical things like shouting our rage and anger into a pillow may help. To release anger I like to go for long walks along a quiet beach and stomp my feet in the sand from time to time.

Letting go of our sense of shame helps us forgive. Shame is very primal as it links into our survival instincts. This goes back to the tribal era when being shamed could mean being banished from the tribe, and this would mean our survival would be unlikely. Shame can go very deep and our inner defence mechanisms against it are very strong, so shame may hide behind denial and rage.

Some of the pain we feel from painful situations is the pain caused by resisting the feeling of "being made a fool of" or "being shown as weak". We may try to deny it and hold back these feelings, as they can be hard to bear. Therefore part of our feelings of being harmed by someone may have to do with the hurtful feelings of shame, which we pile on top of the original hurt.

Shame has a "public" face to it, in that it has to do with how others see us, so sharing our feelings of shame with someone we trust can make a huge and dramatic difference, whether it is ourselves, or someone else we need to forgive. Most of the things we feel ashamed about, such as our weaknesses and foibles and the effects they have on our behaviour are actually common human experiences.

The things we hold inside ourselves as dreadful shameful secrets are very often commonplace experiences, which millions of others have also had in some shape or form. Even acknowledging that we feel shame is a big step as releasing the shame also helps us get reconciled with ourselves and makes forgiveness much more readily achievable. Once we start to bring our dark secrets out into the light of day, mostly they just vanish.

I was recently telling a reliable friend how stupid I felt about a mistake I had made. I had betrayed someone's trust in a very petty way. The feeling had been niggling me for a while, but almost as soon as I said to her, "I felt like such a creep" that feeling started to fade. I could see it did not matter so much after all. There were many good things I had done for the person I felt I had secretly harmed, but somehow those had all got forgotten when I was feeling shame. That one silly mistake had come to dominate my view of myself and while that was the case I could not see myself clearly.

As soon as I expressed the shame it was gone and a more balanced perspective returned. After my confession, my friend went on to tell me about similar things she had done and we had a good laugh at ourselves.

Letting go brings a sense of ease. We no longer need to hold onto how we see ourselves or how we see the other person. We no longer need to maintain bitter and angry feelings. We no longer need to hold on to a feeling of being shamed and unworthy. We may discover that in the larger scheme of things it was not so bad after all. We may even decide that we are not so bad after all too.

Try this:

1. Are there old feelings of resentment, anger or pain you need to let go of? How about creating a regular weekly schedule for a while where you spend an hour getting rid of old feelings and letting them go. Try different methods and see which works best for you. Shout into a pillow, hit a cushion, listen to some sad music and have a good cry, write a letter (but don't send it) to let old feelings out so that you can be free of them. You will feel more able to forgive when you let out the old feelings. Of course, if it feels right, some professional counselling can work wonders.

2. You can also release old stuck feelings by yawning, sighing and groaning. As you breathe out feel as if you are breathing into the feeling and either yawn, sigh, or groan on your outbreath. Start off with a few loud sighs and then try groaning and yawning if they feel right. Letting the feelings have a sound can help a lot so it is best to choose a place where you can make some noise. Do this for at least five minutes and see how it feels. Sighing out loud at times, such as in the car while driving on your own, can help prevent stress building up.

Religion as a Weapon

Forgive those who use religion as a weapon.

Religion seems to be one of the more common justifications for bad behaviour. This can range from the nuisance element of people being "preachy" to actual abuse where people use religion to "justify" violence or emotional cruelty. It is not necessarily the particular religion itself that is the cause of this Religious Abuse, but more the way that people inclined to harm others will use anything as justification.

When we have little experience of genuine love then it is difficult to comprehend the idea of a loving God and what that really means. If we have not truly experienced love then it is easy for us to become fearful and angry. We may not realize that we, "Create our god in our own image": meaning that our idea of God will depend on our level of awareness.

When we are angry and fearful we can become heavily invested in believing in an angry and fearful God. If we then try to preach love, we will do so in an angry and fearful way. Or we may use our religion as an excuse for passive, self-negating, behaviour and be accepting injustices that really ought to be challenged and confronted.

People who are actively religious can become offensive to others without realizing it. They may assume that what they are doing is for the person's "own good" and that they are justified in behaviour, which may be overbearing, browbeating or even violently domineering. If we have been at the receiving end of this kind of negative behaviour it can taint our experience of religion, and also taint our perception of God.

If someone is being hard on us supposedly "in God's name" this can affect how we feel about God. If this happens when we are very young it may be very challenging for us later in life to see God as anything other than a mean and angry being which we would rather avoid. How can we believe in a God of Love if the person who taught us about God was hard and cruel? We need to release ourselves from that experience, so that we can find our own experience of divinity.

Religious abuse will also affect what we believe God feels about us. If we have been treated roughly and told that we deserve it (i.e., we are told that we are "miserable sinners") then we are not likely to believe that we are loveable and acceptable to God just as we are. We may have turned away from our natural sense of religion because of the false version we were offered as a child

If we were offered a religion which lacks in love, or which sets impossible or incomprehensible conditions for us to be loved by God, this can leave a terrible void inside us. We may need to do some serious forgiving so as to reclaim and rediscover our natural religious self – especially if it was smothered with beliefs that are not in harmony with our true nature.

In some religions, forgiveness is a well-established part of the belief system. Yet this belief in the importance of forgiveness can sometimes be a hindrance. If we believe that we "should" or "ought" to forgive, but don't know how to actually do so, then we may feel inadequate and guilty. We may feel unworthy if we feel that we cannot live up to a core principle of our religion – and have no idea where to even start.

While there are many good-hearted, religiously inclined people, some wield their religion as a defence against their fears about life. Such people take a stance in life where they are "special" or "different" in some way. This in itself is not necessarily harmful, but if it fosters a sense of being separate from the rest of humanity then it is definitely harmful. The more separate a person feels the more "special" they need to believe they are in order to compensate.

· · · · ·

One day while enjoying the afternoon sunshine in a park a man came up to me and asked about my religion. Having discovered that I was not a member of his particular church, he tried to encourage me to join. He told me that he was sorry, but that I would end up in hell if I did not do so. After unsuccessfully trying for a while to convince me I noticed that he got less and less sorry that (according to his beliefs) I would be going to hell. In the end, just before he walked away, he seemed to quite like the idea!

The only value I had to this man was to be someone who he could "save". He wanted me as part of his religious bank account! Perhaps he thinks that the more people he saves the higher up he will be in heaven. What an odd way to look at other human beings and how even odder to believe it is "right" to do so. "OK. I'll spend a few minutes trying to save you, but if that does not work I am quite happy for you to go to hell for an eternity." How bizarre. Granted, he is an extreme case, but unfortunately I've come across that same attitude in people from different religious groups.

His attitude made me wonder. What kind of mind likes the idea of other people suffering in hell? What kind of mind can conceive that it would be happy in its "heaven" knowing that others were "suffering for eternity"? Only a mind that could convince itself that "they deserve it", could accomplish this. Whatever they say they believe, such a mind believes in punishment much more than it believes in forgiveness. Such a mind has no real experience of forgiveness, so it cannot conceive it. They literally do not know what they do. Unforgiving minds are invested in unforgiveness – whatever else they claim – because it is all they know. They cannot conceive of life, or even a heaven, which does not maintain their unforgiving stance. They cannot conceive of a heaven unless others are suffering in hell, as that, bizarrely, makes it worth their while.

In my late teens I worked with a man who was part of an obscure Christian group mostly based on the islands off the North-West of Scotland. He believed that his religion was the true one and everyone else was destined for Hell. He would get very bristly if I asked him awkward questions about what happened to Buddhist, or Islamic children who died before ever having heard of Jesus. He always returned to the stance that his particular branch of Christianity was the right one and that everyone else, including most other Christians (who in his eyes were not true Christians), were bound for hell.

Christianity is not the only religion ill-used in this way, but it is the one I am familiar with. I'm sure that many sensible modern Christians would be horrified by this man's attitude. I thought it strange that he could believe that only a select few, from a small island, with a small population, could know the "real truth". For him that was probably part of the appeal. His whole attitude reeked of smug, superiority in the guise of being "humble". Unfortunately this man's attitude is not such a rarity but hopefully it is dying out as we all gain wider experience of people of other religions and beliefs.

Whatever the rights and wrongs of that perspective, it had a very damaging effect on his life. It would have been hard for him to feel a connection with broader humanity while secretly, or overtly, expecting that most of us will be "going to hell for all eternity" – and also believing we deserve it. His only choices were to try to "convert" us, or leave us to what he believed to be our unhappy fate. It is odd that people who believe themselves to be "saved", can be so lost to humanity.

If someone really believes that others are destined for hell and does not feel tremendous compassion for them, and instead feels smug about it, then such a believer is hardly deserving of their heaven. Perhaps ending up in an afterlife with other like-minded people would be natural justice – if not quite heaven! Of course Christianity is not the only religion that gets into this kind of one-upmanship: "I'm going to heaven and you are going to hell." It is the weaknesses in human nature that are the problem rather than a particular belief or particular religion. Often, each side of a religious conflict thinks of the other side as "evil" and "devil worshippers" and use this to justify the horrors they inflict on each other. After all, this mad thinking goes, why treat them well if they are destined for hell? This invisible Hell Industry has been used to justify and create torture, terrorism, brutality and war.

It can be all too easy to fall into the trap of religious superiority, especially as we may have been encouraged to do so by people we look up to and admire. We need to forgive ourselves if we have used our religion to create a sense of separation and superiority towards people of other faiths and cultures. We may also need to forgive people who used their religion in an abusive and aggressive way and in an attempt to control our thinking, beliefs and actions.

Religious issues that may need forgiveness:

- *We may have felt and acted superior towards people of other religions or people with no religion and need to forgive ourselves.*
- *We may have felt offended by people acting superior towards us because of differences in religious beliefs.*
- *Becoming alienated from the religion of our birth by being horrified at the attitudes and behaviours of those who taught us.*
- *Being at the receiving end of judgements and negative opinions for not agreeing with someone's religious beliefs.*
- *Hurt or abused by someone "for our own good" in the name of religion.*
- *Fear of someone else's "righteous" anger.*
- *We may have been bullied into going along with a religion owing to personal, business or social pressure.*

Please note:

In none of this are you being asked to change your beliefs about your religion, but simply to notice the effects of your beliefs on yourself and on others. It is up to you to decide whether a belief serves you or not.

Try this:

1. Have you ever felt judged by a religious person? Have you ever felt bullied by someone with strong religious beliefs? How did this affect you?

2. Do you believe certain religious groups are destined to go to hell? If so how does that make you feel about them? Do you feel superior to them, or do you feel compassion for them? Do you treat them with any less respect, or kindness or consideration because of it?

Forgiving Death

My mother did not die from cancer;
she died from death.

A few years ago my mother died. In one way she died of cancer. However, it is just as true to say that she died from being at the end of her life. She died of death. Cancer was just her way out. In the years before she died she commented to me a few times that she was "a bit tired" and ready to move on to the "happy hunting ground" (she liked to use the Native American description of the afterlife).

Cancer was just the process that freed her from her body. She died from being in a body that was worn out. She was ready to let go of this life. The job of the cancer was to help her to move on. She did not really die of cancer; she died because she was ready for something else.

Just before she died I had an experience of forgiveness with my mum. She was very ill and was sitting on a nearby chair. She was having difficulty getting comfortable. When she moved she was uncomfortable and when she sat still she was uncomfortable. In the midst of this my sister came into the room with some water for mum. The water was in an expensive looking bottle and I made a comment about this, "Oh, that's a fancy looking bottle of water she's brought you mum." My mum looked up at me and said to my sister, "Give him some."

There was something in that moment. In the midst of her discomfort, and in the midst of her knowing she was on her way out, she still thought about me and considered my well-being. This opened me to something I never fully knew before. My mum loved me. I had never really realized that before, as we were never what could be called an openly communicative family. Over the next few days many judgements and resentments I had around my mum just fell away.

I used to judge my mother for not being a good listener. If I was upset or annoyed about something and I tried to tell her about it, she would interrupt me. Eventually I gave up talking to her about things I was upset about. During her last few days I finally understood what was happening. I realized that she loved me so much that she could not stand to hear me being hurt and felt compelled to try and say something to help. She could not stop herself interrupting, as she wanted to help so much. The more I realized this the more all my resentment and judgement towards her disappeared.

Some say there is an opening between the worlds during someone's birth or death. It is said that while a person is in transition between the different realms a bit of spiritual light from higher realms can shine in on this world. That is certainly true of how it was for me with my mum's death, as a simple act of kindness from her, and the atmosphere around her opened me up to a much more forgiving and loving state than I normally experienced.

My mum was an old lady of 82 when she died. I do not think of her as an unfortunate old lady who died of cancer. I think of her as a soul who had grown tired of life in an old body. It is not easy to let go of all we build up over a lifetime. That is perhaps why sometimes the process of dying can seem very rough. The more we hold on to what was and the way we like to think of ourselves the harder it is. This is perhaps what makes things like cancer often seem like such a tough experience. Cancer is not an easy thing to watch in someone you care about and, obviously, often painful and hard to bear for those who get it.

There is no denying the difficulties that such a death brings. Yet there is something else at work in these situations. Near the final stages my mum was being taken care of by my sister in her house. As my mum seemed to be in a lot of pain, the nurses wanted to give her painkillers. She did not want them. They gave her a lecture in how important it was to take the painkillers. She still did not want them. At one point they talked my sister into letting them give my mum the painkillers. Later my mum angrily told my sister never to let them do that to her again.

Afterwards the nurses told me that old people in that situation often don't want painkillers. This suggests that there is something else going on and that maybe sometimes a dying person wants to remain as lucid as possible despite the pain. Perhaps death is at least a bit easier than it looks.

Someone who nearly died from what looked like a horribly painful death offers some surprising insights. The great explorer Livingston was once caught in the jaws of a lion and was being dragged around while the bearers tried to corner the lion to force it to let go. Livingston said he experienced no pain, but was fully aware of what was going on around him. He said he just felt at peace. It was only a while afterwards when the lion let him go that things got painful.

In noticing how friends have handled the death of loved ones I've noticed that they often feel a lot of anger and guilt. The anger may take the form of, "Why did the ambulance not come sooner?" "Why did the hospital not..." and so on. The guilt may take the form of, "I should have...," "Why did I not...." Such feelings seem to be a very common part of our experience around death.

Yet often there is little we could have done, or anyone could have done. If they were really meant to live then they would still be alive. Sometimes clinging to the person who has died takes the form of wanting to cling to their possessions. This may partly explain some of the strange greed that can overcome people around the deceased person's will and arguments about who gets what.

We tend to see death as the worst thing which could happen to us and cling to this life as something which we want to sustain as long as possible. This is natural enough. However, the body becomes worn out and life can become arduous if we try and keep up the same pace and the same type of activities as we did when we were younger. Either we learn to age gracefully, or we fight it and miss out on the serenity that could be ours in old age. Our fears around death make us tend to think of it as bad, yet it is simply unavoidable.

A large part of what we experience in life is out of our control and for most of us the place and time of our death is often one of the things we have little control over.

Try this:

1. If you have lost a loved one, do you feel anger or guilt at the process around their death? Do you blame anyone, or feel guilty from feeling that you should have done more? If so, try saying this a number of times, "I forgive myself and everyone else for the situation around the death of [person's name]. I realize that I cannot change the past and release myself to live fully in the moment."

2. Does death seem like something horrifying to you? It is understandable if it does. However, could you consider that it might come as a blessed release and a sense of going home?

Gratitude, but not as a Platitude

In order to feel grateful for something
we need to have enjoyed it.

Gratitude is often presented as important to leading a happy and fulfilling life. It also contributes to our capacity to forgive and it helps us with being reconciled with ourselves, and the life we currently have. Yet gratitude is not something that can be forced. Wanting to be grateful is obviously not the same thing as actually feeling grateful.

If we do not feel grateful but believe that we "should" then we may feel unworthy, guilty, or anxious about it. We may be worried that we do not deserve more goodness in our lives because we do not feel grateful enough for what we already have.

If we have to pump ourselves up into feeling gratitude, and it is not coming easily and naturally, this means that we need to take another approach. Before we can feel grateful for something there is an important step we need to take beforehand. If we do not take this step then gratitude is virtually impossible.

In order to feel grateful for something we need to enjoy it! If we do not enjoy something how can we feel genuinely grateful for it? If we are struggling with feeling gratitude then it is best to take a step back and focus on enjoying what we have rather than focusing on being grateful. As we have more space to enjoy things we will have more space to feel grateful for them. When we really enjoy things then gratitude springs up effortlessly and easily.

The meaning of the word enjoy is "to make happiness" ("en" means "to make", "joy" means "happiness"). We literally make happiness when we enjoy something. We can enjoy the taste of things, the smell of things, the freshness of things, the colour of things. We can enjoy warm showers, hot baths, and cool evenings. We enjoy whatever things we do on a daily basis, by just noticing the ways in which they make us feel better.

By allowing ourselves to be present for the goodness of even simple things we naturally feel more grateful. We can enjoy something as mundane as drinking a glass of water when we give it attention. We can enjoy our lunch. We can really taste the things we eat or drink. Noticing more of the things that please us lightens our attitude, improves our mood and brings fresh air in to our lives.

Giving things, people and places a chance to please us, gives us a chance to feel grateful for them. Enjoying things does not mean we need to take more time over them – though that really can help. Savouring the things of life may tempt us into adding a minute or two to how long we take to eat our dinner, or drink a cup of tea or coffee. However, just a shift in awareness is often enough to do the trick and help us enjoy more.

Many of us get tempted to indulge in things which are said to be "bad" for us, or cause us to put on weight when we are trying to lose it and so on. However if we are going to indulge there is no point being half-hearted and we may as well enjoy it to the full. It does not help if we mentally beat ourselves up every time we do something that is not "healthy" by then filling our thoughts with stories about how it is not good for us. If we are eating a hamburger, or chocolate, or ice cream then we really ought to savour it and enjoy it rather than dwelling on the downside. It is too late to think about a healthy diet if we are already eating the thing. It is better to get the most out of it, by taking the time to enjoy it as much as we can.

Besides, overindulgence usually comes from switching off our awareness. If we turn on our awareness while we consume something we are less likely to overindulge. We may notice that when we eat too much we really don't taste our food, instead we just stuff it down. If we don't enjoy something how will we know we have eaten it? If we switch to enjoying something then we are switching off our awareness to the signals, which tell us "enough".

Some of the compulsion to overeat may have to do with an inability to fully enjoy food. If we learn to enjoy more then we won't need to eat so much.

If we get into the habit of being too purposeful about life we take all the fun out of it and are much less capable of enjoying it. Being purposeful has its place, but if overdone we can end up feeling too intense and wound up about everything. If we are too focused on some future time and are struggling and striving to be "better", "faster", "smarter", then we cannot enjoy the present because our attention is elsewhere. If our attention is too much on the future, or locked up in the past, then we rob ourselves of the present moment – the only time when we can experience something and the only time when we can *enjoy* something.

One of our deepest needs is to enjoy life. If we become very serious, overly competitive or too wilful then there is little space for enjoyment. When I was first learning to ski I just loved it as it was so much fun. Then I started to get serious and really wanted to work on my technique. I would watch the other skiers and get frustrated as I was not as good as they were. I wanted to get better and better and ski really well.

I soon realized that I was not enjoying skiing any more. The fun had gone out of it as my attention was on technique rather than the joy of whizzing down a hill. I coaxed myself out of my heavy, serious attitude and started skiing for fun again – and I gradually got better at it anyway while just relaxing and being playful.

We have all probably had, or have met people who have had, what we could call a Success-Failure. A Success-Failure is where we achieve successes outwardly, or achieve a goal, but fail to enjoy it. If we do not enjoy something then there was not much point going after it. If it is something we are doing for others, rather than ourselves, we can still get enjoyment from it as we have the satisfaction of doing (or even at least attempting) something worthwhile.

Surely doing something worthwhile is good reason for celebration and being happy? Success-Failures happen when we become so focused on results that there is little space inside us to enjoy the experience.

A forgiving attitude helps us to enjoy life more. We become less driven by a sense of guilt, a sense of bitterness, or not being good enough. We don't feel like we need to make up for something, or escape from something. We can also forgive ourselves and let go of the times when we have been overly serious and a killjoy in our own lives (and possibly in the lives of those around us).

A forgiving attitude helps us be more aware of, and to release, the self-punishment which can so easily be part of being overly driven and purposeful. A forgiving attitude naturally leads to enjoying life more and therefore feeling more grateful for the people around us, and the experiences we have.

Try this:

1. How may things have you eaten but never actually tasted? How many experiences have you had where you were not actually present to really experience them? If you let yourself really taste more of what happens in your life do you think you would feel more grateful?

2. Choose a fruit that you really like to eat. Find a particularly ripe and juicy example. Sit down somewhere quiet where you will not be disturbed and eat it very slowly. Put a small piece of it in your mouth and do not swallow it right away. Let the taste flood through you and hold the fruit in your mouth for a minute or two. Don't swallow until you really have to and just cannot stop yourself. Pause, then try another piece. After you have finished the fruit do you feel grateful that you had it?

Notice how you feel in the next few hours after eating the fruit. Notice your energy level, your mood, and your general sense of well-being.

Addictions and Compulsions

Who is in charge: You, or chocolate?

Many of us do things we wish we would not do. We may compulsively eat sugary or fatty things, drink too much alcohol, become a zombie in front of the TV, or whatever. We may judge ourselves as "weak" or "lacking in will-power", because of this. Maybe we wryly wish that we had more "Won't Power" as the problem seems to be more about what we need to stop doing.

There are also things that we wish we did more of. Perhaps we want to take more exercise, get out more, fix something in our house, and so on, yet, never seem to manage to find the time. Whether we are caught up doing things we regret, or not getting round to things we feel we should do, this unfortunately means that we judge ourselves about it so that we end up feeling even worse.

Forgiveness is very helpful with addictions and compulsions as it is an area where we are likely to feel divided within ourselves. This can cause us to build up feelings of guilt or shame. Any kind of inner division means that we need to reconcile with ourselves so that we can lead a successful, happy and healthy life.

We need to end the battle going on inside us. To do so we need to look beyond our behaviour and beyond our immediate feelings about it. If we feel divided it is because we are pulling in different directions at the same time. This is because we are trying to be different people at the same time.

We all hold and maintain a particular sense of self; a self image which seems desirable to us. This self-image is built up of the ideas about the type of person we want to be. We might see ourselves as "fashionable" or deliberately "unfashionable". We might see ourselves as strong, or clever, or cheerful, or successful, or kind, or steady, as trustworthy, or whatever. As we decide who we want to be, we create a mix out of these as our self-image.

However, the way we would like ourselves to be is not necessarily the way we are now. We may have chosen overly perfect ideas, or have been swayed to try and adapt to ways of thinking, feeling and behaving which are too far ahead of our current abilities. This can cause us to get out of step with the person who we are at this time, and become too idealistic or try too hard. We may be trying to embody characteristics way ahead of our abilities. When we are disturbed by a compulsion or addiction it could be because our behaviour at those times clashes with the type of person we are trying to be.

If we like to think of ourselves as a sensible, intelligent and independently minded person who is in charge of themselves, it can be hard to reconcile this with what we become if a simple thing like chocolate, a sale at the shops, or meeting someone we really fancy, can cause us to lose all sense of control. What happened to our carefully cultured sense of self if a box of chocolates causes us to lose self-control! We may be overcome and not finish till they are all gone, or only the un-chewable toffees are left. What happened to us when we bought that thing in the shops on impulse? What happened to the person we thought we were when we go weak at the knees when we are introduced to someone really "hot"?

Of course, eating chocolate is usually a fairly minor compulsion and has become a bit of a joke. However, there is the underlying issue that part of us is at least a little bit out of control. If we do not think eating chocolate (or whatever our favourite indulgence) is really a compulsion we could try going without it for a week, or a month, and see what happens.

Of course, some compulsions can be very harmful. Addiction to alcohol, addiction to legal or illegal drugs, eating disorders and so on can be the focus of much suffering. Many other damaging compulsions are not so obviously harmful; worry, anger, fearfulness, jealousy, envy, bitterness. These emotional compulsions are less obvious because they don't have a very specific physical action directly associated with them such as lighting a cigarette, swallowing pills, or opening a whisky bottle. However, they can still be very damaging because they affect our health and well-being, creating stress and impacting on our ability to enjoy life.

Emotional compulsions can be the underlying cause of physical compulsions. If we look at our compulsive behaviour we will find a matching inner feeling feeding the compulsion. We may want to eat ice cream when we feel disappointed or sad. We might crave something sweet when our self-esteem is low. We are maybe attracted to certain foods when we feel angry or frustrated. We may even find that for us certain foods are "anger foods", "fear foods", "depressed foods": namely, foods we want to eat when we have particular emotions.

What is the source of these compulsions and the feelings behind them? As we go through building our self-image we get into the habit of pushing down the parts of us that do not fit that image. We naturally tend to filter how we really think and feel. We habitually present a very different image to what is really going on inside us. Over time we reject and repress these parts of us till they go underground. Eventually we forget that we have done so. Compulsions and addictions are an expression of the un-lived (and unloved) parts of us. They are the life force of the rejected parts of us.

Presenting an image of being happy and confident would not fit in with any tendency we might have to being worried, sad, or fearful. However, pushing away feelings, which do not fit with our self-image, does not make them go away. The feelings just go underground for a while and come out in different ways. Our compulsions are fed by the thoughts and feelings we wish we did not have.

If we push something down rather than choosing to heal or resolve, it will only come up in another way. Those unresolved feelings and unhealed parts of ourselves are still alive in us and try to be part of our lives in any way they can, till we resolve the underlying issues. Those parts of us are not bad, they just keep trying to reveal their presence. They have not gone away and they need to be integrated into our lives in healthy ways.

As a child I spent time playing around with the water coming up from a small underground spring near where I lived. No matter what I did to try and block it; small rocks, large rocks, driving sticks into the ground and so on, one way or another the water would come rushing up again sooner or later. When it looked as if I had finally managed to block the flow, within a few seconds, the water would come gushing out behind me or from some other unexpected place.

Trying to repress our nature is like that. We were born with a set of gifts to develop and a set of challenges to work with. If we try and hold it back it will come out somewhere, probably in unexpected places and in unexpected ways. Sometimes the gifts and abilities we have and the problems and issues we face are tied together, so that to gain the gift we need to face the challenge.

Fulfilling our potential includes facing up to things we would rather not deal with, or taking ownership of parts of ourselves which seem undesirable or uncool. The gifts and challenges we have may not fit in with the self-image we have chosen. We may want to be successful in business, but are only focused on finance skills when really we need to learn to handle people better. We may long to be in the public eye, but need to overcome the shame underlying our shyness first. If our self-image is not balanced enough or not complete enough the unexpressed potential within us will constantly challenge us to be aware of our other needs.

The roles we have cast ourselves in may not offer a broad enough range of options to express our wider capabilities. The "tough guy" male, or the butch female, may be repressing their softer side but it has not gone away. The soft male, or feminine female, may have to eventually address the needs of the more dynamic and outgoing parts of their nature.

We can usually see that there is a lot of autonomy and self-direction in the feelings within compulsions. The very existence of compulsions, where we want to stop doing something and cannot, shows that parts of us are struggling to be expressed, independently of our conscious will. When we repress something it still generates feelings. The feelings of loneliness, abandonment and isolation we sometimes experience may well be coming from the parts of us that we have rejected.

In other words, some of our feelings of loneliness, abandonment and isolation come from how we treat ourselves and are not caused by other people. We experience feelings of being rejected, from the parts of us we push away, even though we are the ones doing the rejecting.

We may feel abandoned because we have abandoned parts of ourselves. We may feel angry and not know why because we have rejected a sad and unhappy part of us now reacting in anger to that rejection. We may feel isolated and lonely because we are denying part of ourselves proper expression. We may feel smothered and frustrated because we are denying part of ourselves the right to live. This may seem strange till we remember how much autonomy is behind compulsions and addictions. Part of us has a life of its own, so it has feelings of its own too.

Someone who becomes a sex addict may have unfulfilled longings for deep connections with other people. They may be a stranger to themselves and therefore unable to share themselves in genuine intimacy. We may overeat to soothe anger, sadness or lonely feelings. We may starve ourselves because we judge ourselves harshly and are afraid of losing control. We cannot start a war within us by outright rejection of parts of ourselves and expect to create peace.

Sometimes redirecting a compulsion is enough to resolve it. Other times we might need to look at the emotions which arise along with the compulsion and look at what is really going on inside us. We may be able to shift a feeling or mood by using positive affirmations, relaxation exercises, meditation or music to feel better. We can find ways to work with the feeling rather than ignoring it and hoping it will then go away. It is better to redirect our energy than to try and repress it. If we try to repress something rather than redirect the energy and urges in a more healthy direction then we create an inner battle we are unlikely to win. Who can fight with themselves and win?

Occasionally simple and practical steps will help if no deep issue is behind a compulsion. We can redirect our eating compulsions by redirecting them to something healthier – but it does not have to be something boring. We can redirect to something really tasty and delicious. When the desire for chocolate arises we can redirect it to exotic fruit like mangos, guavas or the like. We are more likely to be successful in cultivating a genuine appetite towards something healthier than just trying to stop an appetite.

Building a healthy sense of self is not just a matter of picking our favourite qualities and deciding that is who we are. That is like having kids and never letting them be involved in what they are going to eat or what they are going to do. Sooner or later the kids will rebel. The parts of us we try to repress are like that; they are like kids who are rebelling and get up to mischief. This is not because those parts of us are bad; it is because they want to live and be expressed.

Our job is to find healthy ways to express them. By expressing them the underlying causes of our compulsions will leave and the compulsive behaviours too.

Try this:

Please remember: It is better to redirect and say "yes" to something else than just say a categorical "no" to something.

1. Next time you want candy, ice cream or chocolate try directing your thoughts into a lovely ripe fruit like mango, peach, pear and the like.

2. Next time you feel a minor compulsion (i.e., chocolate, coffee, etc) notice how you are feeling. Notice anything which has just happened which triggered the feelings. Is there another way you can nurture yourself instead?

Loneliness

*We feel most lonely when we
have abandoned ourselves.*

The pain in loneliness mostly comes from the things we tell ourselves about why we are alone. If when we are alone we have a stream of thoughts along the lines of, "I am no good with people," "It is so hard to make friends," "I will always be alone," and the like, this can make us feel really bad. These thoughts may seem so "obviously true" to us that we do not realize how negative they are; or we can find ourselves trying to avoid facing them as they are so painful.

However, those thoughts are not true at all, they are just negative ideas we have picked up. We may not realize that it is those very thoughts, which are causing us to have the painful feelings that we call loneliness. When we change those thoughts, we change our experience of being on our own to something much more pleasant and enjoyable.

When we run away from painful feelings, or avoid looking at the thoughts that are causing them, we abandon part of ourselves.

Lack of forgiveness tends to make us more vulnerable to the kind of thoughts, which create the pain of loneliness. It also makes us more vulnerable to creating the circumstances where we are alone yet do not want to be. If we have a store of unforgiven material this makes it harder for us to trust others. We also find it hard to trust ourselves as we fear we will make the same mistakes and be hurt the same ways again.

Out of fear, we avoid situations where we would otherwise feel connected and engaged with life. Every time we become embittered by an experience we create "another brick in the wall": the wall separating us from others. It is not the experience which creates the wall, but our reaction to those experiences.

If we don't know who to trust, this usually means we are locked into feeling fearful because of previous bad experiences. It also means that we have not forgiven those who we feel harmed by. Forgiveness helps us gain a detached perspective where we can objectively evaluate who we can trust and who we ought not to trust.

Unforgiveness keeps us in untrusting reactions where we feel that we cannot trust anyone. Perhaps we have judged ourselves as "foolish" or "stupid" if we feel that others took advantage of us. We might be punishing ourselves for our mistakes and teaching ourselves a lesson, by strenuously avoiding the type of contact with other people which we would find rewarding. We may have put ourselves into a kind of social solitary confinement as part of our self-punishment for the mistakes we believe we made.

Not all of our attempts to connect with others will work. People who are socially successful get far more rejections or failed contacts than the social recluse. The socially successful person simply takes it all in their stride as they know that it is a both a numbers game and a learning game. A percentage of their efforts will fail and they will get better at it as they go along.

The socially unskilled person takes any rebuff, rejection, or even just lack of response, far too seriously. They hide for days, weeks or months even after the smallest real or imagined slight. One problem with the attitude of "I'll show them" is that usually nobody notices. They are too busy getting on with their lives (or playing their own "I'll show them" game) to notice. The other problem is that it is really a form of vengeance and therefore part of an unforgiving attitude to life. Like many forms of vengeance it manages to do most harm to the perpetrator.

A forgiving and kindly attitude towards ourselves makes it easier to recover from any unfruitful attempts to have a better social life. While learning what kinds of people we get on with we need to try out different social situations. While doing so our negative beliefs about ourselves, or others, will arise. We can just notice them and not feed them by giving them serious attention.

Creating a good social life is a process of elimination. It takes time to find the right kind of people for our temperament. It takes experience to blend with a new group of people; it is not necessarily something that comes automatically – except for those fortunate ones who are socially gifted. For most people learning social skills takes practise and we can feel odd and out of place in any new social situation until we get used to new people.

In social situations it is often the small things that enable us to turn things around. A while ago I was at the birthday party of a friend and we were all sitting around a table chatting as a group. I started to get more and more uncomfortable, but rather than making my excuses and leaving (as I have often done in the past) I decided to sit it out and see what happened. I noticed how I felt and the thoughts which went along with the feelings: "I don't belong here," "I don't really like these people anyway," "I don't fit in," and so on. Many of them I knew to be good people who I had known for years, so I knew the problem was in my thoughts and not with them.

Someone made a clever comment to the group and my thoughts became, "He always has something clever to say. I can never think of anything clever to say till it's too late." This went on for a while and gradually the uncomfortable feeling started to quiet down. Someone made a lovely comment to the person whose birthday we were celebrating and I spoke out, "Well said. Nicely put." From that simple comment I began to feel like I belonged rather than feeling like an alien.

This is not exactly earth-shattering stuff, but it did allow me to break a destructive pattern which had haunted me for years. I had often felt more comfortable with computers than with people and that experience helped me create a new beginning. It is sometimes in very simple basic things, usually in things we "know" but did not previously do, that major change can come into our lives.

If we are the type of person who tends to withdraw from others when we feel hurt this can make loneliness harder to deal with. The pain of loneliness would make us feel like withdrawing and we could get caught in a loop, which could make us feel very isolated. The way to break out of the loop is to begin to re-establish and widen our social connections. This requires us to release any petty forms of vengeance such as, "They did not phone me so I won't phone them," or "They did not invite me, so I won't have anything to do with them."

It is good to release the beliefs we have about how other people "should" behave. Otherwise we will have unmet expectations which get in the way, "They are not my friend, because they did not...," "If they really cared about me they would...." This kind of thinking leads to building up resentments against other people, which greatly harm our capacity to connect with others.

It helps to remember that an unforgiving attitude not only affects how we see other people; it also affects how other people see us. A genuinely forgiving attitude makes us much more approachable than a surly one of, "What do *you* want?" or a forced half-hearted smile.

Some of us hide away from life as if we are waiting for a Search and Rescue Mission to discover our brilliance and proclaim it to the world. We may be the sensitive type who has trouble fitting in with the roughness of the world. We could be focusing on every slight that comes our way and withdrawing from life in the belief that "Nobody understands me, sniff!", which is odd as most people can easily understand that we are being petulant. Also that attitude means we would be forgetting that we need to "seek to understand rather than seeking to be understood."

The feeling of being abandoned or isolated is the same whether it is ourselves or others who are the cause. If we build a wall around ourselves we will feel abandoned. To end loneliness we need to start breaking down the wall surrounding us. Whatever the bricks in the wall are made of; distorted ideas about how people should behave, overly sensitive reactions, hiding from life, waiting to be discovered, or whatever, we can break out and break through and create happy and healthy relationships.

Forgiveness lets us let go of our rigidity and flow more with life at it is. Forgiveness helps us see more clearly and we are then better able to determine who we can trust, without being held hostage to fear of being taken advantage of, the fear of being rebuffed, or the fear of being rejected.

Pleasant Solitude

The only difference between having a painful lonely feeling and having a pleasant feeling of solitude are the thoughts we think. If we are having thoughts like "Nobody bothers about me," "I am so useless," and so on, this creates misery. That kind of thinking makes loneliness painful and it is really an attack against ourselves. When we do that we have abandoned ourselves to negativity. It would be very cruel to say such things to someone else, and it is no less cruel to say them to ourselves even if it is only in our own minds.

If instead we can have thoughts like, "Time on my own, how lovely. I can just relax and do what I want," "Now I can read that book I been meaning to get to for ages," "I better make the most of this, life will get busy again soon enough." That kind of thinking is not lonely it is simply a pleasant solitude that we can enjoy.

Try this:

1. While doing some regular daily task, such as having a shower, going for a walk, or commuting to work, spend a few minutes gently asking yourself, "How can I be my own best friend?" It's fine if nothing comes up right away, as answers will come sooner or later.

2. When you are alone do you punish yourself with unkind thoughts? Are you ready to let that go and forgive yourself?

The Art of Apology

*Saying "I'm sorry" is not the same as saying
"It was my fault."*

Whether an apology helps or hinders forgiveness depends on the nature of the apology. If the apology expresses a genuine feeling of remorse, or empathy, this can help enormously in the forgiveness process. If the apology is not genuine, but comes from a fear of punishment, fear of vengeance, or spoken through gritted teeth, this will not help much, if at all. If we apologize without meaning it and without accepting what we did was hurtful, it is not really an apology.

However there is a difference between apologizing and being willing to accept blame. Blame is a form of attack. If we feel we are being attacked, because someone is blaming us, it can be a lot harder to apologize as we are being put in a position where we are being pressured into accepting blame. We might feel that we are only partly to blame and the other person might be pushing us to accept all of the blame.

Saying "I'm sorry" is not the same as saying "It was my fault." If a good friend's father dies we might say, "I'm sorry to hear about the death of your father." Obviously this does not mean that we are taking the blame for the father's death. In this case we are using "I'm sorry" to express sympathy or empathy. Acknowledging the other person's feelings is an important part of an apology, but using the phrase "I'm sorry" does not necessarily mean we are accepting responsibility.

Similarly if we say, "I am sorry you feel so hurt," to someone who feels hurt by our actions, they may accept that as an apology even if we do not specifically accept responsibility. Whether that will suffice as an apology largely depends on how we deliver the message. If it looks like we don't really mean it (because we roll our eyes or look scornful) then it will hardly come across as convincing.

The other person may need us to make amends before they will accept our apology. For example, we may need to show them respect if they saw our offence as an act of disrespect. They may need us to show caring and empathy if our original offence was something they saw as cold and uncaring.

It really helps to pick up what it was that bothered the other person and put that in the apology. Using the actual words they use to describe their feelings shows respect and empathy. If they say they felt hurt then we use that word in the apology, "I am sorry you felt hurt by what I said." If they say they felt angry then that is the word we would use: "I am sorry you felt angry about ...." If they are not saying anything then guessing how they felt would at least get things moving. "I am sorry about what I did. You probably felt very upset...."

If we touch someone without realizing that there is a cut or bruise at that point we will cause them pain even though we had no intention of hurting them. Likewise if we touch on someone's emotional sore spot we can cause them pain even though we had no intention of doing so. We can hardly be blamed for this, but some people will not be satisfied until we have apologized for hurting them.

It may be very helpful to apologize even if we don't feel we did anything wrong. An apology is a way of validating and acknowledging the other person. We can feel sorry that someone feels hurt by our actions even if we do not feel that our actions are the real cause. The real cause may be something from their childhood or some traumatic event from their past which has nothing to do with us.

There is not much point in telling someone in emotional pain, "You are just reliving your childhood. This has nothing to do with me," even if that is what they are doing. They are highly unlikely to appreciate that particular insight at that moment! Nor would we be likely to appreciate the way a handy sized object near them suddenly came flying through the air in our direction. Better to apologize and later, when things cool down, help them see the deeper causes.

Unless we are being accused of something horrendous where we feel we were innocent, offering a heartfelt apology can be a wonderful way to help the other person to heal. We don't have to say, "I was wrong," if we do not honestly feel that. We can instead show kindness, caring and empathy.

This shows a willingness to connect and engage with the person even when they are in pain and blaming us for it. This is a wonderful gift we can offer. Going beyond what is right on a factual level to what is right on a relationship level. Apologizing sometimes means forgiving people who are blaming us. We are then forgiving people who don't think that they need to forgive us because they cannot see past their blaming attitude.

A guy I knew was really annoyed with me. He was organizing an event and he wanted me to help him with it. It was a very important event to him, but I felt that I was too busy and refused. Besides, I was going away during the time of the event and I explained that to him. After it was all over he came to see me. He said it went fairly well, but my help would have really made a big difference. I kept explaining to him my reasons why I did not help him, but to no avail. The conversation just kept going round in circles.

Then it dawned on me. He wanted an apology, but did not want to ask for it. I could see he felt hurt and disappointed, but I did not see why I ought to apologize. I had not promised him anything, it was his own expectations, which had let him down. However, it did not look to me like he could hear that.

I focused on how hurt he looked and said, "I'm sorry. You must have felt very disappointed when I did not help you when you needed it. I wish I had found a way to help you, which would have worked well for the both of us. Sorry." He looked very moved and gave me a hug.

An apology may be just the start of the forgiveness process rather than the end of it. A lot more discussion may be needed and some agreements around future behaviour may also be required. For something major there may need to be a mix of forgiveness and reconciliation happening step by step.

As well as challenges around giving apologies we can have challenges to receiving them. We may be tempted to blurt out, "Oh, that's alright..." before the person has even had a chance to finish speaking. Yet it is very important to really listen to an apology. It is best to take a deep breath, make eye contact, and then see how we feel after they have finished.

It could be that the apology has taken us by surprise and we are not ready to forgive the person and do not really want to fully accept their apology until we are more certain of our own position.

It could also be that we just need time to see how we feel and we're not ready to decide what kind of reconciliation, if any, we want. It is important to give ourselves the time we need. Forgiveness cannot be hurried. If someone says, "I hope you will forgive me," we may feel we have to answer. In these situations it is best to wait a moment or two before we answer, or just use a non-committal, "We'll see. I maybe need a bit more time."

Try this:

1. If you need to apologize to someone try and see it from their point of view. How did they feel? If you can, include an acknowledgement of their feelings in the apology, "I think maybe you must have felt [ ] when I [ ]." It might also help to reassure the person about your future behaviour, "I did not mean to treat you with such disrespect. I'll certainly try to be much more respectful of your feelings in future."

2. If you are receiving, or have received an apology, you may want to make sure that your actual feelings were acknowledged. You may want to have a conversation specifically about the event in question. You could say, "Thank you for your apology. I would like to tell you more about how I felt about it." If it is a very emotionally charged issue you may want to talk things over with a friend or hit a cushion beforehand to help you not get into blame or attack mode.

Acceptance

*If we treated a dog the way some of us treat our bodies
we would be arrested for cruelty to animals.*

Acceptance is a quality that supports us being able to forgive. If the idea of being able to forgive feels far away, or unattainable, then acceptance is one of the ways to come closer. If we resist too many things in our life, it becomes a strain, we can end up resenting everything, which does not fit in with our immediate goals.

When acceptance is lacking feelings of frustration and resentment come to dominate. This creates an inner climate that does not help us to feel forgiving. Forgiveness would still be possible, but would not come easily. We end up with forgiveness as yet another item on the increasing list of things we "should" do.

Life may push us to our limit and then beyond. Sometimes all we can do is accept that something happened as there seems to be no way to make sense of it, understand it, or get anything from it. At such times it helps to remember that acceptance is itself a major life skill. Perhaps acceptance is one of *the* life skills.

While it is not exactly something that appears as a requirement in job applications, it is a requirement to make a good job of life. Whatever happens, whatever other people do, whatever we have done in the past, we always have the choice to learn, grow and move on. Acceptance is what enables us to do this.

When we don't have a capacity for acceptance everything feels like a struggle: Everything feels like it is uphill and nothing comes easily. With an accepting attitude we can let life be what it is. We can let things be how they are. Ironically that seems to be when change happens the fastest. Acceptance of how things are does not mean we have given up on what we want; we have just given up getting what we want the hard way. We look for easier ways to get what we want, which involve less striving and less stress. We allow the process of meeting our goals to be as enjoyable as successful results. We accept success as something we can experience now; rather than seeing it as always in the future.

There is a natural flow to life and stepping into that flow feels good. Stepping out of that flow, and working against it, feels bad. Indeed stepping out of the flow can feel very bad. It is when we step out of the flow that life becomes a struggle. We have to push for everything. Nothing moves as fast as we want. Nothing, or hardly anything, moves in the direction we want. It may feel like everything is wrong.

When we are trying to push life outside of the natural flow everyone and everything seems to be working against us. The mail does not arrive on time, people we depend on let us down, and things feel slow or stuck. In those times when it seems that life is working against us it usually means that we are working against life. We are working against the natural flow. To paraphrase: *You can get everything you want some of the time, and some of what you want all of the time, but you can't get all of what you want all of the time.*

How do we know what is the natural flow? Easy. It feels natural. It feels right. A certain amount of effort feels natural; too much effort does not feel natural. Sometimes even a lot of effort can feel natural. However, a lot of effort for a long time does not usually feel natural. It is one thing to stretch ourselves, it is quite another to strain ourselves. It can be fun and exciting to stretch ourselves now and again, or even regularly. However, there comes a time when that stretching begins to feel like a strain and we need to back off a bit till we are ready to stretch again.

If we treated a dog the way some of us treat our bodies we would be arrested for cruelty to animals. This is due to lack of acceptance. We keep the poor thing awake when it really needs to sleep. We set an alarm clock to shock it awake with a loud noise in the morning. We force chemical stimulants (coffee, tea, etc) down its throat to keep it awake and to keep it going when it gets tired. We might not feed it proper healthy food. We may hardly ever take it for walks when it really needs them. Many of us do not even let it live where it has fresh air to breathe, or even clean water to drink.

It is good to ask ourselves, "How does my body feel about how I live my life?" Accepting the limitations and needs of our physical body is part of the art of living a good life. It is essential to accept that our body has legitimate needs rather than treating those needs as various levels of inconvenience. This may be much more important than we realize. The Big Disconnect, the disconnection many of us have with our bodies, is very damaging.

If we are connected to our bodily senses and we have a negative or hateful thought about someone or something our body sense will soon let us know something is wrong. It will simply feel bad to hold such thoughts for any length of time. We will feel those uncomfortable sensations and we can then notice what is going on and change our thinking. If we are disconnected from our body we can harbour the same bad thoughts without realizing how unhealthy they are. We will not notice how awful such thoughts feel and we will not notice the effect they have on our body. Eventually such thinking may turn up as a stress-related ailment or disease.

Acceptance when applied like this is not a vague philosophical idea. It is in the simple, basic and practical choices that we make in our daily lives. The better our sleep time, the better our awake time. Not sleeping properly makes it harder to do everything, including forgiving. How can we forgive if we are too tired to even think straight? How can we forgive if we are emotionally too exhausted to do anything other than switch on the TV and switch off our brain?

It is better to accept our bodily limitations and deal with any sleep issues, and needs for rest and relaxation, as a matter of priority. The better we know what is going on inside us the better we can adjust to life. Pretending something is not present means we are just avoiding it; we are not adjusting to it.

Acceptance of our emotions depends a lot in accepting our body. If we push away our body sensation then the ongoing flow of feelings gets pushed down too, as we experience emotions as physical sensations. If this goes too far we can end up with a sense of numbness. This numbness is only broken through by extreme emotions. Then the subtleties of life may gradually become lost on us and we can only respond to things that are loud, and in our face.

· · · · ·

I went through a time when I only liked flowers that had very bright colours. I could not relate much to flowers with subtle shades and colours; I could not see the point of them! After doing some work on reconnecting and learning to re-inhabit my body I became much more able to appreciate the wide richness of life. I still like very colourful flowers, but now I also appreciate subtleties of pastel tones and the lovely variations of different shades.

Likewise my relationship with my emotions: I mostly tended to notice the more obvious ones like anger, fear, and guilt. At that time I had trouble telling the difference between when I was angry and when I was just frustrated, or resentful. Also the subtle shades of gentleness, kindness, friendliness and compassion also seemed vague and elusive to me at that time. Once I learned to inhabit my body the more subtle shades of feeling became much more real and alive.

Acceptance means accepting our natural limitations and working within them in very practical ways. It might mean doing something as simple as just going to bed early for a while. We could even go to bed early enough that we wake up before the alarm goes off. That would be a much nicer way of starting the day than an alarm shocking us out of sleep. Of course, it might not be that easy. We may have a young (and noisy) family to deal with, or we may live in circumstances where it is not easy to get quality rest times. However, making at least a little effort to accept the natural limitations of our body can go a long way to helping us be more accepting in general.

This brings spin-offs in reducing our levels of stress, resentment and frustration and makes forgiveness much more accessible.

Try this:

1. Notice any ache or pain in your body. As you breathe out imagine that you are breathing into the ache or pain for a few minutes. When ready gently ask yourself, "If this sensation was really an emotion, what emotion would it be?" In this way we accept what is going on inside us.

2. Can you accept the limitations of your body? Would it be possible for you to go to bed early enough to be awake before the alarm goes off? If so, try it for at least a week or so and notice how it feels. You may need to create a night-time routine of reading something pleasant, or listening to some mellow music before going to sleep. It may take a few days or more for the new rhythm to become established.

Forgive the Mega Rich

*If the meek are to "inherit the earth",
then they have to inherit the money too.*

Money is an aspect of life fraught with challenges for many people, especially in these days of financial instability. There has been a rising wave of resentment against banks, bankers, big money corporations, and the mega rich. Although there is probably a fair bit of unhealthy blaming and scapegoating going on in the movement to change the money system it is also a wonderfully hopeful sign.

The reaction against the manipulation of money for the benefit of the few is understandable. However, within our own personal reactions to "the money system" there can be underlying beliefs and assumptions about money which are getting in our way. Our personal issues would still affect us even if the money system were improved. All the "noise" generated by blaming "them" and "the money system" can cause us to miss seeing our own unconscious and unhealthy attitudes towards money.

We are all part of the money system and how it functions. This means that we all, to varying degrees, participate in the dysfunctional parts of it. We may be part of the Arms Trade, and be participating in some dreadful war without realizing it as our pension fund may be invested in weapons companies. The interest we are paid on our money in the bank may ultimately have come from the bank's investment in companies which profit from the tobacco trade, alcohol sales or other activity which we would rather not be profiting from.

Entitlement

Our perspective on money will be distorted if we have a sense of entitlement. Entitlement is always at the expense of others. The rich may feel entitled to manipulate prices and markets to their advantage. The "poor" may feel entitled to manipulate the system too. In the UK, there is the problem of the long-term unemployed who seem to feel entitled to live off the taxpayer for life. This sense of entitlement can lead us to feel that we deserve something for nothing and that society owes us something. If all of us are owed something then who is left to owe anything?

Each of the extremes uses the other extreme to justify their position. The ones at the bottom of the financial pyramid blame the ones at the top ("greedy bankers") and the ones at the top blame the ones at the bottom ("lazy unemployed"). What is really to blame is the sense of being entitled to benefit from society without offering fair value to society.

If our sense of entitlement to money is not matched with what we are actually getting then this can easily turn to blame and resentment. Certainly the financial system should not be manipulated by a small minority for their benefit. However, if we do not resolve our own sense of entitlement then given the chance we would be tempted to become one of the manipulators. We will be carrying a sense of being justified in grabbing our share. We would then be part of the problem.

At the very least unforgiving attitudes about money can block our ability to create the life we want. What we really want has to do with feeling states such as "happiness", "abundance", "well-being" and so on. The more we free ourselves from negativity about money the more easily we can experience those states independently of our actual money situation.

To become financially liberated we need to give up our sense of entitlement and also free ourselves from blame and resentment. We can only contribute to creating a healthy financial system to the extent that we have resolved our money issues. Otherwise our unresolved issues will affect how we see the problem and therefore how we see the possible solutions.

Benefactors

How do you feel about people who are financially better off than you? Do you feel awkward or embarrassed to be around them? Do you feel angry or envious? An attitude, which pushes away people who are more successful than we are, blocks our chances for more success. If we envy the people who are better off than us, then we will block ourselves from becoming like them. If we make someone a target of our ill-will then we automatically block ourselves from emulating them because we will not want to become a target of ill-will. The simple truth is that if we judge someone as "bad" – even out of envy – our morality will get in the way of us becoming like them.

This does not mean that we need to learn to love the bankers and mega rich (though that would be no bad thing) in order to improve our finances. We just need to learn to appreciate those who are at least a bit better off than us so that we can learn from them. This will also make us more accessible to them so that they can help us. Other people will sense it if we are resentful and envious and will tend to avoid us.

Have you ever avoided someone with a bad attitude who you would have liked to have been able to help? The chances are that you have. Most people enjoy helping other people. Those who are better off financially than you, would probably enjoy helping you if given a chance. By "help" I mean a hand up rather than a hand-out. They may be willing to give advice, tips, join you in a business venture, help get you a job interview, or introduce you to good people.

The Root of All Evil

People who are very purposeful, with an intense commitment to a particular goal, tend to "use" other people to fulfil that purpose. If they go too far they will see other people as a means to an end rather than valuing them for their own sake. This distortion even happens with people who have noble goals and they end up caring too much about their project and not caring enough about the people who are helping them with it. What this type of person needs to learn can be illustrated by a paraphrase, "Where there are no people the vision perishes." They need to make sure to care for people; otherwise their project, or vision will suffer.

If someone has "making money" as their primary life goal then this tendency to use people can become particularly ugly. The saying, "The Love of money is the root of all evil" really refers to this kind of attitude. This saying reminds us that using other people as a means to fulfil greed and ambition is the root of evil. When this happens the person loses their sense of connection and caring for humanity. This disconnection makes it easier for them to justify bad behaviour and this puts them on the slippery slope to an immoral end.

Every profound truth has an equal and opposite profound truth. We can actually turn that saying around to being, "The lack of money (to do good) is the root of all evil." Hatred, or aversion, of money by those who would do good with it if they were not so unwilling to "get their hands dirty" leaves a large gap which is filled with those who are only out for themselves. Money being concentrated in selfish hands and not being available to serve the greater good is what maintains many of the ills of the world such as hunger issues. On the level of the individual, lack of money for the basic essentials and for education could also be considered an evil too.

Money is not the Money System

The money system does seem to many of us in need of a good overhaul. However, we need to separate that from money itself. Money, after all, is just paper and metal. Increasingly it is not even that and is often just numbers stored on a computer and presented on a screen.

Money itself is neutral, the money system is not. The money system is designed to benefit some sectors of society at the cost of others. The money system, in its present form, seems to be a mechanism that ultimately concentrates wealth into the hands of a few. Yet, forgiveness needs to be a part of the process of change; otherwise this whole process will further fragment rather than heal society as it stands now.

Attitudes to Money

Some spiritually minded people pride themselves in saying that money is not important to them. I used to be like that, but then I realized how foolish this is. Is food important? Yes. Is having a house to live in important? Yes. Is having clothes suitable for the climate we live in important? Yes. All these important things require money, so money must be important too. If the meek are to "inherit the earth" then they have to inherit the money too, for it is money that shapes what happens in the world.

Spiritually minded people who eschew money do themselves and the world a great disservice. We need the money in the world to be more in the hands of the good people of the world and less in the hands of the greedy and the selfish. The money system will only change when a different and more caring group of people have control of money and use it for the greater good.

The capacity to create money has been largely centralized in government and banks. We are seeing some small changes to this through other forms of value being generated by individuals. Local money systems such as LETS schemes, time dollars and other similar systems have had some success. We are also seeing value being generated by individuals online. Facebook "Likes" have value, Linkedin endorsements have value and the "gold" won in some online computer games have been sold for real money.

We are seeing electrical power generation become less dependent on a centralized system as more individuals have the capacity to generate electricity in their home. We are far from the point where we can pay for our shopping with Facebook Likes, but there is a definite trend at work. The individual is becoming less a consumer and more of a direct creator or generator of power and value. However, as much as we might like to see fundamental changes in the money system it is not likely to happen overnight. In the meantime we can look to improving our own attitudes to money otherwise we will be contributing to things staying the way they are.

Our attitude to money can be filled with contradictions, complications and ambiguity:

- We may believe that no one should receive money unless they have worked to earn it. Yet, we may hope that house prices will go up so that the value of our home will increase even though that would be money we did not actually earn.
- We consider ourselves as generous and willingly give to others. Yet we may also be poor at receiving and thereby not give others the chance to express generosity.
- We may believe that fair exchange is only right and proper. Yet, we might begrudge every penny we have to spend.
- We may believe that we like money yet we may hardly ever look at the currency notes that we handle daily. What images are on them? What is written on them? What colours?
- We could be bemoaning the injustice of the present money system. Yet, we may take every chance we get to take advantage of those injustices where they serve us in our lives.
- Thinking of money as dirty, yet we may resist letting it out of our hands either by spending it, or by giving it away.
- We may believe that money is not important to us yet we may be very envious and angry about people who have more of it than we do.
- We might believe that money cannot buy happiness yet we may try and get as much money as we can anyway.
- We may say that it is better to give than receive; but, do more receiving than giving. Are there any churches that don't do that?
- We may be Eco-poor in that we do not enjoy the money we have out of excessive fear or worry about the impact our activities will have on the ecology of the planet.
- We may have lots of money, but be poor in heart and derive little happiness from the act of living.

Try this:

1. How do you feel about the money system and those who operate it? Can you see any areas where forgiveness would benefit you?

2. How do you feel towards people who have more money than you?
   How do you feel towards those who have less money that you? Do you
   have any attitudes towards those with more money than you, which block
   your success?

Men and Women

"He is so annoying. He does everything I ask him
to do no matter how ridiculous!"

Very few people get through the process of finding a life partner without experiencing rejection, disappointment, or some form of unrequited love along the way. We might also have had guilty fantasies about someone who was involved with someone else, such as the partner of a friend, colleague or even of our boss. Hopefully we will have had times of delirious happiness and celebration in the search for the love of our life, but even so most of us do not get through the process unscathed.

Even the people who seem to have it all, and also seem to be able to have just about anyone they want, will have a sad story or two that they could tell. To add to the challenges, some of us have a quirk in our nature causing us to feel most attracted to people who are the most unavailable. The whole business of finding a life partner offers many opportunities for both having to reject someone and also for feeling rejected. This area of life is very ripe for forgiveness.

One of the most confusing times in relationships seems to be the dating phase, when we first get out and about meeting members of the opposite sex (or whatever is our gender preference). All our hormones are afire and yet we are unlikely to have developed the skills we need to negotiate our way through the situations that we will experience. The scars from this time carry over into life's later phases. Many hopes, desires, assumptions, and beliefs can be severely tested at this time as we have our first few trips on the roller coaster of relationships.

• • • • •

I asked Tania, who is a very attractive young woman, how it was going with her new boyfriend. She looked a bit hesitant, so I asked what was the matter. "Well..." she said, "He is so annoying. He does everything I ask him to do no matter how ridiculous!" I would have laughed if she had not sounded so upset. It turned out that Tania was trying to get the measure of this guy by pushing him to see if he would stand up for himself. He was just not getting the message and was assuming that the more he did to please her the more she would like him. When actually the more he tried to please her the less she liked him.

She eventually ditched the guy. It was a bit sad really as I think he was probably in love with her (or at least infatuated) but did not know that falling over himself to please her was – paradoxically – not going to please her. She totally lost interest in him, and any feelings of being attracted to him, because he behaved in too many ways, which seemed to her to be unmanly.

Tania is a modern, educated, highly intelligent women, yet she was having a hard time relating to a guy who was going out of his way to please her. In relationships our instincts come into play and our instincts are not politically correct. Sexual attraction is based on the "voltage" which comes from opposites attracting each other. Tania may like a guy who is very considerate of her feelings, but if he overdoes it her biological computer will not identify him as a potential mate. She will then lose sexual attraction to him and he will end up in Just Friends category, at best.

This sort of situation is not unusual, as I have come across many similar stories when I operated an online dating site. This kind of misunderstanding causes confusion and upset on both sides. The guy was certainly not happy with the outcome. He thinks he did his best and got rejected for his efforts. The harder he tried the worse it got. Tania was not happy about it as she lost attraction to someone who she was attracted to initially, and did not know why. She got upset because she felt disappointed at the outcome and confused about her own reactions. She was worried that there was something wrong with her as she had finally met a nice guy and ended up not being attracted to him. "Why am I only really attracted to jerks?" was her plaintive question.

If one of the people in the relationship tries too hard it usually puts the other person off. It is so common that we have to pay a price for "trying"; we could call it Trying Tax. To avoid paying Trying Tax we simply need to avoid going too far and going too fast. Relationships take time to develop. It is nice to make an effort for someone, but too much begins to feel like pressure to the other person. It is good to buy someone flowers and chocolates, and give them lots of treats yet, too much too soon and the person feels like they are being bought and will not like it.

We also pay Trying Tax in the later phases of a relationship too. One person may withdraw from the relationship a little to take some space for themselves. This happens from time-to-time in the natural cycle of a relationship. The other person may react to this by falling over themselves to please their partner.

This can cause the partner to lose interest – if it is overdone – because they just need a bit of space and are not getting it. If there are other things to keep them to-gether, such as kids, they may stay in the relationship, but a lot of the spark will be gone unless they can balance the relationship again. Sometimes couples will take turns paying Trying Tax. One withdraws, the other pursues. The pursuer gives up, then the one who had withdrawn becomes the pursuer. And so on.

It is important not to be too hard on ourselves for the mistakes we make in relationships. Much of the problems we face especially in the dating phase (and more especially our first time in that phase) is our lack of skills. It is not that there is something wrong with us, it is just a lack of skill in learning how to handle potential life partners. Some believe that we should know how to handle the op-posite sex by instinct. They say that, "It should all come naturally." Even if there is some truth in this, instinct is not enough on its own.

• • • • •

A cat is an instinctive creature, but it spends all its time as a kitten practising how to be a cat. While a kitten is at play it is practising for its role as an adult by play fighting, playing at stalking and so on. Similarly a dog spends its time as puppy practising being a dog. Animals have all the right instincts yet spend their forma-tive years in practice, practice and more practice.

We cannot expect to learn the significantly more complex task of developing the social skills needed to become a well-functioning human being without need-ing a lot of practice and without making a lot of mistakes. Our mistakes, some of which may make us wince when recalled, are all probably a perfectly fine and normal part of the process of learning the skills necessary to function as a human being.

As an answer to our relationship challenges a well-meaning friend may have told us, "Just be yourself and it will all work out." The problem with this is, which "self" are they talking about? Such advice is usually useless as we all have many ways of expressing ourselves and finding the right self for the job is part of learn-ing about how life works. It is like learning to drive a car: we want someone to show us what to do and not have to learn by crashing all the time.

Part of the challenge in relationships is that the other person may be doing and saying things simply to test us. Tanya, in the above, was testing the guy to see how he would respond. "Would he stand up for himself?" was what she wanted to know. This tendency for what we could call Interpersonal Testing is a survival instinct at work. Rather than taking years to get to know what someone is really like we can test them to see what happens.

I've noticed that I sometimes use joke comments to test people. If I have a hunch that someone has a big problem with a certain issue I'll maybe make a joke somewhere vaguely around that theme to see how they respond. I've asked a variety of people whether they test potential partners and many of those who admit they do respond with a laughing, "Yes!" as if to say, "How did you know?" Others deny it vehemently, which just makes we wonder if they are hiding something.

It takes more than a few decades of social change to compensate for the thousands or millions of years-worth of instinctive responses, which sit ready to be awakened in a modern human being. Those instincts will be there, especially when they have to do with something as important as finding a mate.

A wise female in ancient times would want to know that her male partner will not desert her, and their child, if a wild animal comes charging into the village. Her instinctive self will probably cause her to be sexually attracted to strong male energy, and to reject potential mates with weak male energy. When survival is at stake who wants a nice understanding guy, who is too sensitive to kill anything, when you can have a rough and tough character who will bring home some meat?

Certainly we have moved on from those times, but that does not mean that all our instincts have moved on too. If a woman is not sexually attracted to an overly nice guy, as seems fairly common, it does not mean there is anything wrong with her. It does not mean she is "only attracted to jerks". It just means she needs a nice guy who is connected with healthy male energy rather than a guy who is uncomfortable with his own male energy and is rejecting it, or avoiding it. It is good that many modern males want to get past outdated male stereotypes like the "macho man", but we must not turn ourselves into females in the process. Such men need to stop reading the likes of *Men are from Mars and Woman are from Venus* for a while and get out and generate some testosterone.

The changing roles of women can also surprise us. The world would likely be a better place if women became more assertive and we had more females in leadership positions. However, this needs to be done by women taking on healthy forms of assertiveness rather than copying the same distorted forms of assertive behaviour which immature males express.

I was heading into Glasgow airport a few years ago in a taxi. The taxi was driving at the speed limit on a motorway when another car, a typical "boy racer", quickly overtook us. I commented to the taxi driver, "Goodness, he was going a bit too fast." To my surprise the driver said, "He? It might not be a he. Ever since the Spice Girls era the young girls are driving just as fast and crazy as the young guys." We already have enough people on the planet acting out immature assertive behaviour.

Hopefully women who want to be more assertive can find mature ways of doing so, rather than copying the mistakes of us males.

Try this:

FOR MEN

1. Do you have strong views about "Women" and how they need to change? Think of as many ways as you can and write them down. Look at your list and for each item ask yourself, "How can I change so that is no longer an issue for me?"

2. Are you an overly Nice Guy who usually ends up as friends with women even when you want more than that? Can you forgive yourself and create a healthy positive relationship with your own male energy so that you can move on?

FOR WOMEN

1. Do you have strong views about "Men" and how they need to change? Think of as many ways as you can and write them down. Look at your list and for each item ask yourself, "How can I change so that is no longer an issue for me?"

2. Do you know an overly nice guy trapped in a relationship with a woman friend (including yourself), which is not going to go anywhere? Can you find a way to help point him towards creating a healthier connection with his male energy?

BOTH MEN AND WOMEN

1. What was your worst experience of rejection, or unrequited love? Try spending a few moments thinking about the self you were then and what you wished you had known which would have eased your anguish and upset. Imagine going back in time and whispering this new knowledge to that unhappy part of yourself and see yourself as you were then brightening up and smiling.

2. Can you laugh about the mistakes you made when trying to find a mate? If not are you now ready to begin to see the funny side and thereby forgive yourself and move on?

Sex for Higher Purposes

Celibacy cannot be the answer for everyone
as soon there would not be anyone.

As a culture, our ambiguity about sex shows up in the way that so many of us get obsessed by it, yet many words associated with it are considered to be swear words. In looking around the web for all the swear words that I could find, in order to set up a filter to block their usage in a dating site I was running, what I discovered is that there are a surprising number of them. A large percentage of swear words relate either to the act of sex or the bits of our bodies we use for it. We live in a culture obsessed with "being sexy", yet, many of the words used around sex are considered "dirty".

I first heard about sex as a topic when, as a very young boy, another boy announced, "Do you want to know how you were born? Your mum and dad were fooling around in bed. That is how you were born!" At the time, I just assumed he was an idiot. Whatever this "fooling around in bed" was all about I was sure my mum would never do such a thing!

When I got a bit older and heard more of the actual details about what is involved I felt a mix of fascination, disbelief and hilarity. "What! We are supposed to put our boy thing into her girl thing and do what? You are kidding! Right?" For a long time I wondered, "Why would anyone want to do that?" Much later as I was approaching puberty I found a sales catalogue with pictures of ladies in swimming clothes and underwear and started having all sorts of strangely compelling dreams afterwards. After that the topic of sex seemed much more interesting.

Sex as a Spiritual Practice

There are schools of thought that look to use sexual energy as a means to become enlightened. This is a very appealing approach, especially when compared to the "sex is sinful" angle many of us grew up with in the West. Western religious leaders seemed to assume that we would all decline into endless debauchery if not kept in line by being taught to believe that sex was wrong in some way. Yet, many other cultures have high moral standards without having to resort to packaging sex in guilt and shame.

Seeing sexuality as something which can contribute to our spiritual growth feels a much healthier approach than one, which puts us at war with the sexual part of ourselves. There are some rather dubious "gurus" around who seem to use teachings about sexuality as license to get their hands on as many attractive followers as they can. However, as long as we approach the topic with common sense we can avoid the more questionable approaches and gain tremendously from exploring other approaches to sexuality.

It is important to bear in mind that exploring sexuality as a means to spiritual growth is not the same thing as exploring sexuality as a form of "thrill seeking". The two may sometimes overlap, but there are ways in which the two paths definitely diverge. Sexual energy is a potent force and approaching practices like Tantra with the same attitude with which we would approach an amusement park (looking for bigger and bigger thrills) can lead to serious problems.

If we seek more and more intense experiences then we can actually be narrowing our awareness rather than broadening it. To create intensity we need to have a narrow and specific focus on something. However, the development of spiritual awareness needs to include an opening and a broadening at some point in the process. If we are addicted to intensity we will miss out on the broadening part and get out of balance.

Tantra has an understandable appeal to many Westerners owing to its open and explorative approach to sexuality. It is very attractive to be able to step free of the guilt and shame around sex and be able to see it with a fresh view. Yet the effect of learning Tantra, like any subject, depends on how it is taught. Wise Tantric teachers adjust their teachings to suit the Western mind and Western attitudes. They offer a balanced teaching where intensity is used to help people experience the fullness of life without their concepts and assumptions getting in the way; along with the a sense of spaciousness and openness which allows those experiences to be integrated into daily life.

Much of the attraction of sexuality is that it gets us "out of our head" and into another experience of life than our thought processes. However, going to the other extreme and overly identifying with the body and its energy is not the answer either. We don't want to go from being stuck in our head to being stuck in our genitals. We want to know ourselves as the deeper and wiser part of us, which enfolds and embraces all the aspects of our life energy in a harmonious way.

Sex is not the problem

It is relatively easy to maintain our integrity and stay true to our sense of morality when it is only lightly tested. When the stakes are higher and it is something we really want that is when the true test comes. It is in facing and handling such tests that our character develops.

The problem with sex is that sex is not the problem. The problem with sex, if there is one, is what we will do to get it. It goes like this: You want something very intensely. What will you do about it? Will you negotiate or will you manipulate? Will you lie, cheat, hurt, steal in order to get it? Will you be open, honest, kind and caring even if you are not sure that will get you what you want? Will you hurt someone (financially, emotionally or physically) to get what you want? The more we want something the more we are tempted to adopt dubious methods to get it, if it is denied to us. These are the challenges which sex faces us with.

There are two very different kinds of temptations when it comes to sex. One is a physical temptation; the other is a spiritual one. There is a pressure to meet a desire; yet there is also a pressure to behave in line with our morality. It is in learning to handle the spiritual temptations of sexuality, and do the right thing under pressure, which develops our spiritual capacities. It is the qualities that we develop in relation to our sexuality which determine whether it is part of our spiritual development or not. If we do not bring spiritual qualities to our sexuality then it is not part of our spiritual development and it is a lost opportunity.

The physical temptation and the spiritual temptation of sex are obviously closely related, because if the physical temptation were not present there would not be any moral or spiritual issues either. Learning control of our physical desires helps shape our growth as individuals. It is an obvious part of fitting in with society and developing our character. Yet too often the physical temptation is assumed to be the issue when it is really just the mechanism to deliver the spiritual opportunity – such as choosing to be caring and considerate in the face of the temptation to "use" others.

Celibacy

For some, celibacy works. Yet, that is obviously not the answer for everyone. Celibacy cannot be the answer for everyone as soon there would not be anyone! If a person becomes celibate to avoid the issues created by sex then they are also avoiding the issues created by life. As a way of getting clearer around the issues a temporary celibacy can be a good thing, but eventually the underlying life issues need to be faced.

Sometimes a person is so fully engaged in a creative project that their sexual energy naturally tends to sublimate. When that is the case sexual energy transforms gracefully without staunch denial and the associated frustration that can arise in trying to block it. It is better that energy is diverted rather than blocked. Trying to block sexual energy through an act of will seems to eventually pervert the energy and create more problems than it solves – as many in celibate religious orders have discovered.

If someone finds a way to have all the sex they want, but treats everyone concerned with an open, honest and caring attitude, who can really fault them? (Except out of envy?) Someone else might mostly avoid sex, but be resentful about it and becomes devious and manipulative in their occasional attempts to meet their needs.

Such a person will see sex as a moral problem when it is their willingness to manipulate others that is really their moral problem – sex is just the mechanism that highlights it. They will have similar attitudes and behaviour in other parts of their life. Sex serves to make our issues more obvious by outlining them in an extreme way.

Many issues; feeling unworthy, wanting power over others, feeling a victim, and so on can all come up in relation to sex. Such issues get magnified by the pressure that sexuality brings to our life force. Anything that blocks or distorts our life force will become more intense when something increases that life force. Sex obviously increases our life force. Sexual attraction speeds up our evolution by placing our issues in stark contrast.

Sex and Kindness

The ancient mariners always tried to navigate by stars to get them through stormy or unknown waters. With the issue of sex it behoves us to have a star to be guided by. The "star" I suggest is kindness. How often have you seen the words sex and kindness used together? Not very often I suspect. Yet, we sometimes call sex "making love". If that is true, would that not include kindness?

Bringing kindness into a situation raises it up to a higher level. We talk to a stranger in a kindly manner and they might end up a friend. We can be kind to the person at the checkout counter and they are likely to feel a bit happier. We can think kindly of the person who overtakes us rather recklessly while driving and at least we will feel better.

Likewise consciously bringing kindness into sexual activity helps to lighten and freshen our attitude to it. It is also the type of approach that more truly makes sex part of our spiritual practice. Being kind and considerate to our partner is more naturally part of our spiritual development than being able to stand on one leg, and chant an obscure mantra while having sex. Any genuine spiritual teacher would say the same. It is about attitude as much as it is about actions.

If kindness does not seem sexy enough to you then try another quality such as respect, consideration, or even boldness or courage. Having a specific quality we are choosing to focus on around sexuality helps to offset any tendency for unconscious feelings of guilt, manipulation, exploitation and feelings of inadequacy to get in the way. Bringing in an ennobling quality, ennobles the experience.

Porn

I dealt with porn a lot when I was running a dating site. My website had a "no sleaze please" policy, but people would still insist on trying to put porn and links to it in their profiles. What I noticed about porn is how easily it can become very tedious, especially when having to look at it when not in the mood. After all most porn movies have basically the same ending!

There is a wide debate with many people having big agendas around the issue of porn. Some argue the damage it does; some argue that it has some benefits. The only thing, which nobody disputes, is that it has been around a long time and that it is easier to find than it used to be.

What if porn, and our attitudes to it, are a symptom of something deeper?

What kind of person does *not* need porn? Would a healthy and well-adjusted person ever look at porn and if so in what ways? Is porn good for some people? Our assumptions about porn show in how we answer this kind of question.

If someone is leading a rich and full life are they less likely to be heavily into porn, or more likely? My guess is that someone who is leading a rich and full life is probably less likely to be interested in porn. This suggests that the more heavily someone is interested in porn the more this indicates that something in their life is out of balance. There is something unfulfilled and unexpressed in their current lifestyle. It could be simply sexual frustration, but it could be more than that.

Human beings evolved with a connection with the natural world. Indeed our survival depended on that connection. Owing to our prevailing techno culture, sexuality is for many people the last remnant of that connection to nature. If we expect sex to provide all of that connection it has the same effect as expecting one person to meet all our needs. It is expecting too much.

Our thinking processes can help to liberate us; yet our thinking processes can also ensnare and trap us. We can be so caught up in our minds that life becomes sterile and lacking in depth. It is like watching an old black and white TV. The mind gives sharpness, but if we overdo it life can lose its colour.

Sexuality is an invitation to reconnect with the primal and the primitive. It offers a much needed contrast to experiencing life as a thought process. There is a tendency in us to become separate. Sexuality pushes us to connect. Handled rightly it offers a healthy balance. Handled wrongly it leads to another extreme.

The problem with porn is that so many people get so heavily serious about it. There are many good reasons for this, but it often has the effect of feeding the guilt and shame cycle. If people feel guilt and shame about their sexuality it is harder to find healthy ways to express it. They are then more likely to become secretive about it and more likely to find an outlet in porn. If they feel guilt and shame from looking at porn this feeds their sense of having to be secretive, and so on.

If we detach and take a step back from it, porn can start to look quite funny; bits of bodies wobbling around and people making strange grunting or hooting sounds with odd expressions on their faces. If we can see a funny side to it we are less likely to become obsessive and less likely to become addicted. This may seem to some to be trivializing porn addiction. However, it is almost impossible to become addicted to something that makes us laugh. Taking it so seriously is what makes people vulnerable to becoming addicted to it.

Obsessing and enjoying are not the same thing. If we become obsessed we tend to lose our sense of enjoyment and get entangled. Bringing a form of genuine enjoyment back into something, by at least lightening up about it, begins to set us free again. After all, levity is a quality of spirit; gravity is a quality of matter.

The real problem with porn is the loneliness and isolation that is behind it. It is the sense of disconnection that leaves people prey to overly investing in a part of themselves, which offers at least a thread of connection with others.

Sex Solution

I used to say that if I had an on/off switch at the back of my head, which I could use to switch off sexual energy, I would switch it off as I did not want to bother with it. I eventually learned better, but for a long time I felt it made life too complicated. Now that I am older I am more in need of a volume control rather than an on/off switch – some way to turn it up when I need a boost!

There is no need to separate our spiritual nature from our sexuality. Nor is there any need to try to convince ourselves that the act of sex is in itself somehow "spiritual". We make something spiritual, or not, depending on how we approach it and what we bring to it. What makes something "spiritual" is the spirit (intentions, attitudes, feelings, beliefs) that we bring to it. If we try and make sex into a spiritual practice we miss the point if we focus just on physical technique, or if we focus too much on ourselves. Neither does avoiding sex necessarily make a person more spiritual especially if it means they are avoiding important life challenges which they need to learn from.

Becoming an adult does not mean becoming just a bigger version of a child. It means transforming from one sense of our self into another. Anything that encourages self-obsession in the form of too much concern about "my pleasure", "my desires", "my energy", just inflates the infantile self and does not develop the adult self. We transform our sense of self into being an adult by becoming more aware of others and by finding a place in the world. Similarly, we transform our sexuality by expressing our caring and compassion through it, not by solely focusing on the technicalities of sex as the pseudo gurus would have us believe.

Try this:

1. Do you need to forgive yourself because of feelings you have about your sexuality?

2. What spiritual quality do you most need to bring into your attitude to sex?

PART FOUR

Advanced Forgiveness

Forward Giving

Forgiveness is something we are
rather than something we do.

In this section we explore some of the more advanced ways of looking at forgiveness. We will explore more deeply some of the themes we looked at earlier, such as releasing a sense of being a victim, releasing the need to blame, and so on.

In learning advanced ways of looking at forgiveness we begin to move beyond seeing forgiveness as simply releasing a desire to punish. We begin to see forgiveness as an ally in helping us live our life more richly. How we see other people changes too. More and more we see other people as being on our side. They seem like they are on our side, because we are choosing to be on their side. Choosing to be on their side puts us on the same side. We lose some of our fear and replace it with wisdom.

Forgiveness becomes less of something that we do and more of something that we are. We develop a natural empathy for the feelings of others and this makes it much easier to see things from their point of view. This also makes it much harder to judge people and much harder to hold anything against someone.

A useful way to explore the deeper aspects of forgiving is to think of it as "FORward GIVING". You may have heard of "give forward", and this is a similar pre-emptive way of living. We learn to see the world through a more forgiving pair of eyes. We stop seeing forgiveness as something we do after an event, and begin to see it more and more as something we do before the event. Forgiveness becomes an attitude we carry with us wherever we go. Forgiveness eventually contains, surrounds and enfolds all the experiences of our life.

In our initial way of approaching forgiveness we may have seen it as a way to handle feelings of being hurt or harmed. In Forward Giving we see ourselves as having co-created our experiences. We take more responsibility for our own reactions to our circumstances and put less responsibility on others. We can do this because we have learned to stop blaming. When we stop blaming ourselves it becomes much easier to accept the ways in which we are responsible for our life, as we do not need to fear our self-judgement. When we stop feeling the need to punish ourselves we no longer need to hide the truth from ourselves and can accept our weaknesses and foibles with a kindly smile.

When Less Forgiveness Is More Forgiveness

When we stop blaming others we feel no need to punish them either. Often we find that *we do not need to forgive because we felt no desire to punish*. We become more focused on learning and growing from the events of our lives, and less focused on blaming or shaming. We become more interested in helping and healing the people we meet and less interested in creating and maintaining our own personal drama. We end up having less need to practise forgiveness as we no longer have to use it to deconstruct the judgmental and blaming attitudes we used to maintain.

With forgiveness everyone becomes our teacher and everyone becomes someone we can teach. Even small acts of forgiveness can go deep. I well remember a small incident from my childhood where I learned about forgiveness from my mum showing me an example of how to do it. We lived in a bottom floor apartment, and there was a metal pole near our front door that went up from the ground to the bottom of the balcony of the flat above. My brothers and I used to climb up that pole, but one day we got a stern warning from our parents to not do it any more. Apparently when we climbed on the pole our neighbour upstairs could hear the sound coming up through his floor and it was annoying him.

One day I could resist temptation no longer and was most of the way up the pole when my mum came out the front door and saw me. She did not shout or get angry with me, she just looked up at me and gently said, "Come down son." I climbed down and she kindly patted me on the head and said nothing more about it. I was so surprised about not getting into serious trouble that I never did climb that pole again. My mum's response somehow made me feel warm and safe and that it was alright to make mistakes sometimes.

It also made me a bit more forgiving of people who get caught breaking the rules than I would have been otherwise. Later when I would catch someone out I would find myself remembering that small incident, and how much I benefited from feeling forgiven, and would tend to be easier on them than they expected.

In each and every situation we are either teaching forgiveness or we are teaching unforgiveness. Forgiveness does not mean that we cannot set clear rules and boundaries. Some situations call for having very clear rules with clear consequences for breaking the rules. It just means that we value the person more than the rules. We allow a genuine desire of wanting the best for the person, and the best for everyone else involved, to guide us rather than be guided by a desire to punish. Every time we practise forgiveness, or at least make an attempt to forgive, we teach forgiveness. By our efforts we influence others, in ways which we may not be aware, to be more forgiving.

The best kind of forgiveness is when we completely avoid the need of it. Those are the times when we are operating in harmony with the deeper laws of life. When we have a forgiving attitude we tend to have a wiser attitude too. It is like we are living on a higher altitude and can divert potentially hurtful events with greater skill and grace. If someone is argumentative with us, rather than reacting and arguing back, we can look to what they really want and then look for a mutually acceptable solution. We don't need to argue against someone, because from a forgiving state we want them to get what they want. We just need to find a way where we can get what we want too.

A Forward Giving attitude allows us to intervene before our own harmful reactions take over. We may even be able to transform a potentially harmful situation into a pleasant experience, or at least a neutral one.

· · · · ·

One New Year's Eve a big drunk guy came lurching up to me cursing, and swearing loudly, and obviously spoiling for a fight. I was cornered, so I could not do the really brave thing and just run away (there is no merit in fighting with a drunk).

I wondered, "Oh, oh, what do I do now?" as I saw this big mean-looking guy get closer and closer. Then suddenly I knew what to do. I found myself shouting at him with a mix of aggression and compassion, as I bellowed, "What's the matter! Are you alright!" He suddenly stopped short like he had hit a wall and rocked back on his heels. He looked totally dumbstruck. He had no idea what to say and looked really confused. Then I said to him, again in a strong, but kind voice, "Careful here as this part of the street is icy and really slippery." Just then a neighbour appeared on the scene, but by then the would-be attacker was emotionally disarmed. Much to my surprise this big guy who a few moments before looked like he wanted to attack me ended up leaning against the wall and sobbing uncontrollably.

This same method can sometimes work even with animals. As a young boy a dog suddenly came running up to me snarling and growling. Then, I had an idea. I called out to the dog in a friendly voice as it ran toward me, "Come on boy... Come on... Good dog... Good dog..." and bent forward as if I were greeting a very friendly dog that I was glad to see. The dog stopped short in front of me and also stopped growling. It lifted its head to the side as if it were confused for a moment, then started to wag its tail. I noticed it seemed friendly at that point, so I gave it a gentle pat on the head and it ran off.

Forgiveness is part of a bigger picture. It is part of a deeper and wider perspective of life and events. Forgiveness can become proactive and enhance our lives by allowing us a greater capacity to shape events so that we bring greater harmony into our lives.

Try this:

1. In what ways would a more forgiving attitude make your life better?

2. What do you teach most often, forgiveness or unforgiveness? Which one is the most fun to teach?

Turn Tormentors into Mentors

*How the people who challenge us the most
can help us the most.*

When it comes to handling people who we find particularly challenging there are many ways in which forgiveness can help. The people who challenge us the most also offer us some great opportunities to gain in wisdom, insight and strength of character. To gain value from our tormentors we first need to admit that they exist. If we believe that it is wrong to dislike or hate other people it can be hard to fully face up to our own negative reactions.

Yet it is in facing those reactions that we give ourselves the best chance for deep and lasting change. If we react against someone, we might feel that we are being unfair, we may feel guilty, or we might feel afraid of what will happen if our true feelings become known. We are putting a brave face on it and pretending that everything is fine or dismissing the extent to which we are finding someone challenging. We may have a boss, a colleague, or a relation, who we cannot stand, but in order to "keep the peace" we push away our feelings and pretend it is all alright. After a while this becomes a habit and we lose connection with our true feelings.

On the other hand we may feel that we are justified in our feelings and that we may make the mistake of taking our reactions at face value. We might decide that we hate someone because they are hateful and must deserve it. We may be covertly taking vengeance on the person through backbiting, gossip or doing harm to them any chance we get. Or we may be openly at war with the person and things have descended into a mutual hatred where each person sees the other one as the baddie and that each person believes their harmful behaviour is justified by the harmful behaviour of the other. "Well they started it..." is the huffy justification of both infants and adults.

In the course of life we will meet people who we will feel intense dislike or even hate towards. It might be our inner warning system telling us to beware, but it can also be a reaction that has nothing at all to do with that person. They may remind us of someone or something that we cannot bear to think about. The first step is to be honest with ourselves about our reaction, but without acting out our feelings in harmful ways towards the other person. In the privacy of our own heart and mind we need to accept and admit to ourselves how we feel and ask ourselves how we can find a better way of responding.

Our true character shows not in how we treat the people we like, but in how we treat the people that we do not like. It takes practice and skill to handle strong negative reactions wisely. It takes skill and experience to accept such reactions, yet hold them in abeyance, so that we always treat others with respect and decency. Repressing a negative reaction to someone may be useful in the short term, but in the long term we need to resolve it if we can. Acting out the feeling of dislike would just cause more damage and cause them to dislike us in return.

If we feel intense hate towards someone and we habitually push it away we may end up rejecting the part of us which hates. We may reject part of ourselves out of hand because it brings up such uncomfortable feelings, without exploring what it is offering us. It may be trying to protect us from someone or from something bad happening to us. Hate, although it can be very intense, is just a feeling. It is an intense sense of rejection or revulsion toward someone or something. Such an intense response can teach us something very useful if we learn to handle it wisely.

Having a hateful reaction to someone offers us wonderful opportunities to heal the hateful, spiteful, vengeful part of us. To handle those feelings we need to "raise them up" and not try to "rise above them". Often the attempt to "rise above" is really an attempt to escape the challenges of intensely uncomfortable feelings.

We need to get past the fear that our deeply negative feelings mean that there is something basically bad about us. They are just feelings that we need to learn to work with. We can work with them if we connect with them and not run away from them, or be swept away by them.

· · · · ·

Some years ago I worked with someone whose behaviour I detested and I judged him as being very pushy and arrogant. Jerry was the kind of guy who tried to dominate every meeting. He stole my ideas and then presented them as his own, he was always boorishly trying to be the centre of attention and so on. More than one colleague told me that Jerry was the most arrogant individual they had ever met in their lives.

I was well on my way to hating Jerry, but I also felt strongly that I wanted to try and find another way. I could also see that having other people agree with me about how bad Jerry was did not offer any real solution. I wondered if I could set aside my personal reaction and somehow learn something from the challenge of getting on with Jerry. I was not ready to leave that job because the work itself was really interesting and fulfilling. I decided then to try and find a way round the problem.

Life can be a mirror and other people may present us with a mirror-image of our attitudes, beliefs and behaviour. People who are our opposite, whom we may find easy to react to and to detest, are simply offering us the other side of the picture. This got me to wondering whether Jerry was mirroring something useful about myself. Perhaps he was expressing something, in a distorted and out-of-balance way, which I ought to be expressing.

I asked myself, "What qualities does Jerry have that I lack?" At first I could not think of anything good about the guy. But after a while something dawned on me. Jerry was very bold and confident. He was always very upfront about what he wanted and never left doubts about what that was. He often got out of balance with how he expressed those qualities, and his boldness too often became arrogance.

However, there was no denying that he did have those qualities of boldness and courage. When I looked at whether I was expressing those qualities I could clearly see that I was not. Rather than being bold and confident I was being cautious and circumspect, especially when confronted with Jerry. I realized that to rise to the challenge Jerry was offering me, I would need to develop the qualities he was expressing: I would need to become more bold and more courageous. I could also see that those were the very qualities I needed to develop to become more successful in my life. Too often I had played a back-room role and I needed those qualities to break out of that.

I began to see that Jerry was offering me a real gift. He was confronting me with qualities of character I most needed to develop to make a success of the next stage of my life. This realization made it easier for me to begin to forgive him and to judge him less harshly. I began to realize that when I was building up a hatred of Jerry I had been building up a sense of guilt and duplicity too as I was having to hide how I truly felt. I could now begin to let go of the hate and the guilt. I began to see my tormentor as being my mentor – even though he was not aware of his role.

Jerry was mentoring me in how to be more forthright and direct with people, whether he knew it or not. I took steps to develop the qualities of boldness and courage which Jerry so abundantly expressed and began to put myself forward in situations where previously I had held back. I became more upfront with people and less shy about saying what I wanted and what I intended.

One day Jerry came into the office and I looked him in the eye in a way I had not done before. I somehow knew right then that I had learned what I needed. Soon afterwards life moved on and an even better job came my way.

The willingness to forgive and to see the best in people offers practical advantages and opportunities to become more empowered. Our enemies, protagonists, and those who are just plain annoying, may be offering gifts to us by confronting us with what we need to develop. Our tormentors may really be mentors in disguise as they demonstrate the qualities we need to add to ourselves to become healthier and more balanced people. They may well not be expressing those qualities in ways we would chose. *Nevertheless it is the character qualities we need to look to not the behaviour.*

This helps liberates us from purely personal reactions and see the bigger picture of what is going on in our lives.

Try this:

1. Think of someone who antagonizes, annoys or upsets you and ask yourself, "What positive character qualities does this person express that I lack?" Are they bold, courageous, assertive, sensitive, caring or what?

2. How would your life be better if you expressed the positive versions of the qualities of your "tormentor"? How can you learn to express those qualities?

Learning by Teaching

Those who can't preach;
those who can teach.

As we become more active in forgiving, and see the benefits it brings, we will want to share what we have learned with others. Forgiveness is better taught by example than by getting preachy with people who really might not be all that interested. We teach forgiveness by forgiving ourselves and by holding a forgiving attitude towards others.

However, there is another way we can "teach" forgiveness. If we see someone behaving in a way that is likely to cause them a lot of suffering, we can choose to do a Forgiveness Intervention. Usually a Forgiveness Intervention would only be done with someone we know fairly well, such as a long-term friend or family member. A Forgiveness Intervention is intended to help the person break out of a destructive pattern.

John, a friend of mine, had a habit of falling out with people. In fact, he seemed to be the sort of person who was not happy unless he had an enemy at hand. One evening John was complaining bitterly about a mutual friend, Robert. John had just fallen out with Robert and was giving me a detailed account of what happened.

Just as John was running out of steam (or possibly just pausing for breath) I intervened. I spoke in the same disparaging tones he was using about Robert, but used very different words. I said, "Yeah, that Robert. Remember the time he tried to fix you up with that beautiful French lady you had your eye on? Who does he think he is! What kind of friend would do a thing like that?"

While I said this, John's body language changed completely. He lost has belligerent attitude and put his head in his hands. He than looked up and said with a wry grin, "Oh the guilt, the guilt...." and then he had the decency to laugh. John felt so bad about it that he made amends with Robert, re-establishing the friendship the next day.

Another example is when Stephen, who I had known for many years, complained bitterly about his ex-wife Anne. This was not the first time I had heard him talk like this, so after listening for a while I asked him what was the worst thing she ever did to him. It was when they were working together in one of the world's trouble spots. It was physically a very dangerous situation, with bullets flying around and they had agreed not to start a family till they moved to somewhere safer. Anne very much wanted a family and, without telling Stephen, she stopped taking the contraceptive pill. When Anne got pregnant Stephen was furious about it and felt that she had been devious and irresponsible.

Their daughter, Jane, was about seven by then and I knew that Stephen really doted on her. I said to him, "It looks to me that Jane is one of the best things in your life." "Yes!", he agreed emphatically, that his daughter was very dear to him and that he could not imagine life without her. I followed up with a question. "Does that not mean that the worst thing which Anne did to you, turned out to be the best thing which has ever happened to you – the birth of your daughter?" Stephen just went quiet, and as that was rare for him I said no more. Stephen did not have complete reconciliation with his ex-wife, but things did seem to go smoother between them. I did not hear him complain about her so much after that.

My friend Pete, was visiting me. Pete had a habit of complaining, especially about the government or some other "they" or "them". He would complain that the government should not do such and such; that the government should do this and that instead, and so on.

He started complaining about some of the events around a funeral that both he and I had attended a few weeks before. There had been people there whom he wanted to avoid. He hated Martha, with whom he had had a long and bitter quarrel. Because I had had enough of him complaining and partly because I was feeling a bit touchy around the events of the funeral too I did an intervention.

He complained about Martha being at the funeral. I said simply, "The funeral is in the past. You cannot fight with the past and win. She was there and that cannot be changed." He complained about some of the horrible things Martha had done to him in the past. I said, "You cannot change her behaviour and you certainly cannot change what she has already done. You can only change how you think and feel."

His complaints about Martha continued and he said the mutual friend who brought her to the funeral should have known better. I said, "Do you think Martha would be happy that you are upset?" He answered, "Yes, you bet she would. You know what she is like, she is not happy unless she is bothering somebody!"

I said, "Well, why jump into the hole she dug for you? She maybe only went so as to annoy as many people as she could. All the more reason not to get upset by her."

Every time he got into feeling upset I contradicted him with simple points which he could not, or would not, want to argue with. Eventually he quietened down and we shifted onto talking about other things. I knew that he had a long drive ahead, so as he was leaving I offered him some positive thinking CDs to listen to on the journey. He happily accepted and later phoned to thank me for them and for our conversation. He has been much more positive and empowered since then.

All of these interventions involved people I knew well. I knew them well enough to know a bit about their story and where they were contradicting themselves. Also, they all knew in one way or another that I was their friend and that I was on their side.

It is possible that similar interventions might work with people we don't know well. However, the interventions might also come across as being rude. The less well we know someone the more we need to make sure that any intervention we do is gentle and kindly – this is always the best way anyway. As we get better at doing interventions with others we will likely get better at doing them on ourselves too.

When we find ourselves caught in a bitter, resentful or angry loop we can notice what is going on in our mind and contradict our thoughts with simple facts about not being able to change the past and so on.

Try this:

1. What are the typical rants that you get into and what are they about? (Ask your friends if you don't know what they are.) What could you say to yourself to break the pattern?

2. Do you have a friend or family member who gets into rants? Is there a kindly way you could help them to break out of it? Would any of the above examples work with them?

Turning Complaints
into Intentions

*It is better to ask for what you want
than complain about not having it.*

Complaining is not usually a forgiving attitude; it is more usually a blaming attitude. It often involves wanting to place blame on someone or somewhere. Complaining can be an expression of long term resentment, which is oozing out in whatever way it can, or it could just be annoyance at a short term inconvenience. Either way, complaining is usually a sign of an unforgiving state and that the unforgiving mind is at work.

Victim feelings are usually supported by thoughts along the lines of, "They should do something about this!" "Why is this happening to me?" "Why can't they get it right!" "I'm not shopping here again!" and so on. Such thoughts usually have the theme of "someone has done something to me."

Underneath the complaining is a feeling of being disempowered and having to resort to anger, blame, verbal attack and other expressions of unhappiness to get what we want. This is different from a confident attitude of being dissatisfied with something and happily negotiating for something better. It is also the difference between feeling "insulted" or indignant about an event rather than just seeing it as a possible mistake that has been made which will be willingly corrected as soon as it's pointed out.

I had a new girlfriend visiting me and as we were driving along in the car she started complaining about this and that in the relationship – mostly about things she felt I should be doing. As I listened to her I realized that I had no idea that this person had wanted the things she was complaining about not getting. My forgiving mind must have been active for instead of reacting I just said, "It is better to ask for what you want than complain about not having it." She looked startled, and went quiet. After that, she did get better at asking for what she wanted.

A complaining tone of voice sounds victimized. The voice tone may be of an angry victim rather than a hurt victim, but either way it is still a victim tone. When we use a victim tone of voice we signal "this is your fault" towards those we assume to be the source of the problem. The other person will pick up on that message no matter the words we actually use. That simple switch from complaining to asking can change everything in a person's life. The feeling we get from someone's whining, "Why don't you ever?..." is very different from the feeling we get from a positively expectant, "I would like..."

I was feeling very low one day as I was going through an experience of unrequited love. I felt like complaining and I plaintively asked, "Why does this keep happening to me?" Much to my surprise I got an answer. Out of the blue I had an insight. It was like a very kindly presence saying to me, "*It's because you are being stupid.*" It came as a bright flashing insight and there was no judgement or malice in it.

I looked up the word "stupid" in the dictionary to get the exact meaning (to do with "*not thinking clearly*") and realized that was exactly what I was doing. I was just not thinking properly and was not really clear about what I wanted. I was trying to create a relationship with people who were not available and I needed to think first, and explore the relationship for a longer time before building up hopes and expectations.

There is a huge difference between, "Why is this happening to me?" and "How can I get what I want?" One speaks of being at the mercy of life; the other speaks of affecting life in ways we choose. The two approaches also get very different responses from other people. With complaining we might get what we want, but it is at the expense of the relationship. This may not matter if we just want a refund from a shop, but if it is our life partner habitually complaining it may result in grudged giving, "I better, or he/she will complain," and growing resentment.

Asking directly for what we want allows more negotiation to take place so that one person is not giving over what they want to a complainer, "just to shut them up" (as if it ever really does that). There may be a happy compromise when both sides are willing to negotiate. When there is no negotiation there is no happy compromise and it is a win/lose situation. The complainer "wins", but often at the expense of the other party as their needs have not been taken into account. The complainer is usually only focused on their own needs.

The challenge is to be willing to be vulnerable enough to ask for what we want. If we want something and have doubts about our worthiness to receive it, it will be a real challenge to find a way to come right out and ask for it. Saying it directly may feel scary. They other person may say "no" to our request. Perhaps we fear that they will confirm our worst beliefs about ourselves if they do.

It is not so much the saying "no" to a request that may hurt us, but the apparent rejection and apparent invalidation of our value, which would hurt. The other person may be oblivious of how important it is to us for them to say "yes", so we let them know in advance by putting an emotional charge in our asking.

We may be subtly warning them that we will be upset if they refuse us. This is not negotiating our needs in a healthy way. In doing so we are avoiding dealing with any underlying sense of not deserving or negative beliefs about getting our needs met. These can only be healed by being more conscious of our needs and expressing those needs more openly (when safe to do so) with the relevant people.

Many of us get stuck in complaining habits in childhood. As children we are initially totally dependent on others. Our survival depends on getting others to meet our needs. At first we do this without words; crying, whimpering or whining noises and so on. Later we learn to be more specific by using words. However, we may still use the same tone of voice we learned when we were very young.

Within someone who is whining (even if angrily) there can be a sense of them expecting to be refused. Some on the receiving end may react with a knee jerk "no" and refuse out of hand; others give way but sometimes with feelings of ill will and of being manipulated.

Somehow along the way, many of us have come to believe that just asking for what we want does not work so we stop ourselves doing so. If we grew up in a large family with many mouths to feed, and especially if resources were scarce, we learned that "The squeaky wheel gets the grease." We perhaps saw others get what they wanted, while we were ignored. We probably noticed what the successful ones did to get what they wanted. Perhaps we learned to display some form of implied threat or manipulation to get what we want, "If you don't want me to cry/get angry/be upset..." In other words, we learned to "squeak". This habit can become so ingrained that we hardly ever notice when we are doing so in our present daily life.

By shifting from an attitude of complaining to one of intending to get our needs met in healthy ways, we uplift our basic approach to life. When we do this we are confirming to ourselves that our needs are important as we are taking them seriously and looking for healthy ways to meet them. In a way we are promising ourselves to look after our needs. If we follow through on this promise to ourselves we then grow an inner sense of reassurance. We then get the feeling that our needs can and will be met. This makes it even easier to step out of complaining and into intending.

Complaining, unless it is done with a positive attitude (then it is more like negotiating than complaining), holds us in a negative and disempowered pattern of relating. Looking to what it is we really want and how to express our needs in positive healthy ways create a more forgiving climate in our inner world. We can release resentment and disappointments from old unmet needs and not carry those feelings into present day situations. Forgiving ourselves and forgiving the others involved frees us to move on emotionally and take a bolder approach to life. We can be more confident and self assured when we know that our needs are respected. The person who most needs to respect our need is ourselves. If we do not take a positive approach to our needs, it is unlikely that anyone else will. If we associate rejection or denial with a present need, owing to past experience, then we are living in the past and need to forgive and let go those old feelings.

Try this:

1. If you habitually complain is there anything underneath that you need to release and forgive?

2. When you want something do you negotiate openly and happily? Do you mostly "cry" (complain) for what you want, negotiate for what you want, or create what you want?

Ideals, Hopes
and Expectations

*The job of our idealistic self
is to be 'unrealistic.'*

Our ideals and expectations have a lot to do with how we relate to the world
and to other people. How we handle our expectations can make the difference between a happy life and one filled with misery and disappointment. If we
expect "10" and get "8" we will be disappointed. If we expect "6" and get "8" we
will probably be delighted.

How we manage our ideals and expectations also affects how we relate to ourselves. Particularly it affects how we relate to the part of us that generates those
ideals and expectations. If we allow that part of us to run riot then we will be
expecting too much from the person or situation. Not only does this set us up
for disappointment, it can eventually cause us to mistrust the source of creativity
within us which is generating those hopes and expectations. Our creativity is the
foundation of our aliveness so mistrusting it means mistrusting parts of our core
nature.

It is not these creative energies that cause us to be disappointed (when things
don't work out); it is our unwise handling of them that is the cause. Creative
energy is by nature fluid and flowing. Its job is to go beyond the bounds of current situations even to the point of being "unrealistic"; it is our job to direct this
energy in the appropriate way.

If we become bitter and try and repress this energy out of mistrust we alienate
the part of ourselves that helps to give life meaning. The healthy expression of
our ideals and expectations allows us to unleash our potential and create new
possibilities for ourselves and for the world in which we live. In learning to handle
our ideas and expectations we need to learn to forgive ourselves as well as those we
feel have disappointed us.

Part of our need to forgive others comes out of our expectations of how they ought to behave and what we feel they should or should not do. If someone behaves in a way where we feel hurt or disappointed, is that necessarily their fault? It could be that our expectations were unrealistic and that the other person did nothing wrong. On one level we may still need to forgive them, as we need to release our desire to punish. On another level it could be us who has the problem because it is we who has got upset or angry.

In some situations nobody did anything to us, we did it to ourselves. Who is responsible when we get upset? We don't really know the answer to that until we look deeper and see why we are upset. We need to sort out whether we had unrealistic expectations, or whether they broke an agreement, or the like. We cannot always assume that just because we are reacting to someone that they have necessarily done anything wrong. We need to question ourselves, rather than just making assumptions about other people.

If we feel disappointed it may be because we may not have communicated our hopes and expectations to the other person. They could be cheerfully oblivious to what we actually want because we have not expressed this clearly. Perhaps our expectations are unrealistic or inappropriate for the person or the situation. We may be holding on to fantasies from childhood and comparing our life partner with a Prince or Princess from a fairy story, or to a parent from the overblown perspective of a small child. It may even be that our hopes and expectations are just too unrealistic for any mere mortal.

They may have very different ideas from us as to what behaviour is right or proper and we could find ourselves feeling badly let down simply due to a misunderstanding.

If we are looking for a life partner, or a business partner, we need to be careful not to start building fantasies and assumptions around potential matches. If we get disappointed because the person will not, or cannot, deliver on our expectations we may end up feeling that we need to forgive them. However, were they ever really at fault? Was it not our expectations that were the problem and not the other person?

It is fine to have hopes and dreams, but we need to be cautious about building them around other people too soon. Otherwise we end up having to rebuild ourselves after having our hopes dashed. When this happens, of course, it is important to forgive ourselves. However, it is also important to look at the root causes of this behaviour pattern. The root cause of the behaviour is a deeper pattern of thinking and feeling to do with needing to build a healthy relationship with our own idealistic self.

We may have an innocent, imaginative, and childlike self, intervening in how we live our lives. This self does not know what is possible, or what is not possible, it simply generates ideas that we need to learn to evaluate and adjust to the world in which we live. Sometimes we may find the ideas presented by our idealistic self to be so lovely and compelling that we miss out the evaluation process entirely and take on board the ideas just as they are.

If the situation goes awry (the potential partner does not return our calls, the business fails, etc, especially if this happens a number of times), we may be tempted to mistrust the idealistic part of ourselves and blame it for our disappointments. However, the problem was not with our idealistic self as it was just doing its job to open us to possibilities. The problem was we did not evaluate the possibilities properly and got swept away by the moment.

Our idealistic self is trying to alert us to possible answers to our needs and wants. Our realistic self also needs to be involved in the process so that we can evaluate whether those "possibilities" have merit. Our idealistic self is only offering us partial information. We need to fill in the picture with what we currently know on a practical level. When this does not happen we are blindly acting on partial information and can eventually damage our relationship with our idealistic self as we can end up feeling that we cannot trust it.

We need to be able to contain our idealistic self (or rather the needs and drives behind its ideas) without repressing it. The answer is not to become mistrusting of this part of ourselves, or to become cynical about life. The answer is to accept this part of us and to help it grow and mature. As we help it mature this part of us can be a valuable aid in lifting our life to a higher level. Rightly handled the idealistic part of us offers a power source of creativity to help us create a happy and fulfilling life. Wrongly handled the idealistic part of us will lead us to create many disappointing and heart-rending situations.

Some things which arise will be just fantasies and not at all achievable in the world as it is now. However, these too have can have value, especially if our response to our creative self carries a feeling of, "Yes, wouldn't that be wonderful. It's fun to play with that idea, but I don't think we can do anything about it."

Reclaiming our creative drive, including the ways in which it expresses itself in our ideals, can go a long way to helping us be reconciled with ourselves. By being more conscious of our expectations we can step out of blaming others for not fulfilling those expectations and learn to negotiate for what we want. We not only learn to negotiate with others we also can learn to negotiate with ourselves. We learn to make sensible trade offs such as trading some of our need to be responsible and committed with some of our needs to be free and spontaneous.

Try this:

1. Are you aware of a situation where you experienced pain and disappointment and you felt it was all or largely your own creation? Did you fall
   into self-blame and self-judgement about it? Did you feel less trusting of
   yourself afterwards?

2. Imagine what it would be like if you harnessed the juice of your creative
   abilities and channelled these in really practical ways. Imagine one part of
   you playfully producing a stream of possibilities and the other part of you
   happily shaping those possibilities into realistic goals. Imagine what it is
   like to have your idealistic and practical selves working together to improve
   the quality of your life and the lives of those you care about.

Creativity

*Learn to think outside the box and you will soon
think yourself out of the box you were living in.*

Unleashing our creativity is an excellent way to create the best possible relationship with ourselves, with life, and with others. When you explore your creativity you are exploring yourself. You will find new capacities and abilities, which you did not even know you had. Life takes on a lighter tone, becomes easier and far more fulfilling. Events take on a new meaning as you see them as a chance to develop and test your new-found capacities. Problems become a lot less of a problem when we see them as opportunities to be creative and find workable solutions.

If you have a problem in your life where you are not sure what to do, take a step back from it. Imagine ideas popping into your mind and you having a sense of knowing what to do next. Do this a few times and you will soon find a solution that never occurred to you before. You find a number of ideas come to mind and you can play with them, ponder on them and combine them to find the best way forward. This turns you into an active creator of your life and circumstances. You turn a problem into a gift.

You had a problem and what you got from it was a better connection with your creativity. When you connect with your creativity you connect with deeper parts of yourself.

Perhaps the only reason that problems exist is to give us a chance to become creative, to reach deeper within ourselves and find untapped resources which enable us to handle life better and better.

Our creativity is not only expressed in artistic projects, though obviously that can be part of it. It is expressed any time we make an effort to find a creative solution to a problem, or to reshape something in our environment. It is important to see creativity as a natural part of our daily life even if we are not artists as such.

Creativity has its part to play in everything from making a nice meal, working in the garden, solving a problem at work, or finding new ways to have fun.

The more we unleash sparkles of creativity the more life sparkles and becomes enjoyable. We find new ways to work, new ways to socialize and new ways to play.

Many of us have a book we want to write, but hold ourselves back. Perhaps we are worried that no one else will read it, or it will be rejected by publishers. However, writing a book, or any project of that scale, is as much about honouring our creative capacities as it is about success in the world.

The process of writing a book, if we write from the heart, awakens new perspectives and awakens our creativity. If you write a book and nobody else ever reads it, it is still worth writing it because of what the creative process gives you. Your ability to handle life will have expanded. This is especially true if you follow your own flow and write what you feel like writing rather than write what you think you should write.

There is never any justification in putting yourself down or beating yourself up for lack of external success. Besides, nowadays, we can always get our work out by putting it on a website. We can just give it away if we want to make sure someone else benefits from it. Expressing our creativity is an honourable endeavour that enriches our inner life, independently of externals. Yet sooner or later, in one way or another, our external life will reflect our enhanced creativity, as the external must ultimately yield to the creative.

If we are hankering to write a book, or some other project, but there is no way we can realistically do this in the foreseeable future then it is best to examine our motives. If our motives have more to do with ego than something we genuinely want to offer to others, then it is best to just let it go. Otherwise we risk weakening ourselves by using up our life energy on wishing for something that is unlikely to happen since we are not fully behind it. This will free up our creativity to flow in fruitful ways rather in being frustrated because it is directed towards the impossible or the implausible.

I still have occasional longings to be a world-famous rock guitarist. Since I am now in my late fifties, hardly ever practise guitar and don't even have a decent amplifier, it is not likely to happen! Since my motives are not exactly high, as I tend to feel that "want to be a rock star" longing when I want attention, I don't let my lack of progress in that area concern me much.

Expressing our creativity brings a new-found sense of freedom. We are not limited to just fitting in with the life we find ourselves in. Our creativity shows us ways forward, around and through our difficulties and challenges. More than this, our creativity shows us how we can contribute to life and make the world a bit better. We get business ideas, ideas for inventions, ideas for how to live a better life, ideas for how to improve our relationships. We see things less as problems and more as opportunities as we feel the "juice" of our creativity rise up when we face new challenges.

The more that we use our creative abilities the more we learn to trust them. The more we experience ourselves finding solutions to the issues we face the more we know that we can always find a way forward. Our confidence in our capacities and abilities grows and evolves and we can easily handle things, which previously we would have found daunting.

Honouring our creativity by giving it prominence honours our deeper self. We are no longer limited to the person we thought we were. We are bigger, bolder and wiser than we realized. The person we thought we were was shaped by those around us in our formative years. We are not limited to that. Those people may have limited themselves in unkind ways, and placed the same limits on us. We do not need to do the same. We can develop and express our creative potential in whatever ways we choose. As we learn to think outside the box we think ourselves out of the box we were living in too.

If we find ourselves with time on our hands this is a gift to use to develop in new ways. We can explore new topics and develop new skills. We listen and learn. We practise becoming more observant and notice things we did not notice before. Out of that capacity we then notice a wonderful opportunity right in front of us that we had not seen before, and we seize it.

We learn to listen better, really listening to what others are saying and making sure we understand them fully by asking them questions. Then we notice that we are really "hearing" people much better than we ever did. We feel more connected to them and to life. We see ways in which we can help them deeply as we can see their deeper needs and we respond to their needs in creative ways. We have more we can offer, so more is given to us in return.

If we do not express our creativity and it is burning within us, this can lead to deep unhappiness and bitterness. Thwarted creativity is our life force turned against itself. We *must create something* as it is intrinsic to our nature. If we don't respond to urges to create something good then what we create will not be good. We will then create destructive relationships, repeated failure and endless problems. We cannot deny or suppress our creativity without denying what is best about life. We cannot deny our creativity and expect to have well-being and abundance.

Our creativity is the source of the abundance within us. It is through contact with our creativity that we can do the most to contribute to the world and enhance our experience of life.

Try this:

1. Take a few moments to notice and acknowledge the ways in which your creativity already enhances your life. Have you recently had an idea or impulse, which made a situation turn out better? Notice this kind of experience more so that it can happen more often.

2. Do you feel a strong creative urge, which you talk yourself out of acting on? What feelings do you have which stop you acting on it (fear, embarrassment, feeling overwhelmed, low self-esteem)? Is there any way you can express that urge even in just a small playful way?

What if I Chose It?

Even if you believe you have no choice,
claim back your power by imagining you do.

There is much evidence to show that those who recover the best from painful events are those who find something meaningful in the experience. In our formative years, we tend to look to others to help us understand the world and to help us see the meaning of events.

Afterwards we tend to make the same assumptions as those around us as we were growing up. If we do not learn to question those assumptions we could be still be applying other people's assumptions to our current life circumstances and these may not be useful. Our assumptions may be blocking our ability to find meaning in the kinds of experiences that challenge us.

We all have experiences that we find difficult. Yet we know that other types of people may simply breeze through exactly the same situation. Whether we find something easy or difficult has a lot to do with the assumptions we make about the meaning of an event, or the meaning of someone's behaviour. If we feel confident we may interpret a new experience as an opportunity. If we don't feel confident we may experience it as a threat. When we respond differently, we get different results.

We can learn to change our assumptions and change how we interpret events by loosening up our habitual ways of responding. We can break out of our well-worn pathways of thinking and feeling and learn new ways. The new ways may feel a bit odd at first, but they will give us a wider range of options for our thinking and feeling. We will have more choices in how we interpret and experience the events in our lives and so are more able to adapt and respond in life-enhancing ways.

The exercise below helps us tap into our inner wisdom and to see events and circumstances from a different perspective. It is a way to find meaning in what otherwise might seem to be baffling or meaningless events. We can use this technique for past events or current situations. We allow the item to come to mind then ask ourselves questions like, "What if I chose it?" and "Why would I choose this?"

You do not need to believe that you actually did choose it, as that is not the point. You are not being asked to believe anything. The exercise is not about what you believe, or what you don't believe. The point of the exercise is to create a frame for your thinking, which strengthens your capacity to find hidden meanings and hidden insights about yourself and about life. The exercise also helps you break out of your normal way of looking at things to be open to new ways of thinking, new ways of feeling and new ways of responding. It helps make your mind more flexible: like a form of mental yoga.

The exercise works even when it does not provide any useful answers immediately, as you will probably not be able to think of the situation in quite the same way again. Your thoughts and feelings about it will be more fluid. If the exercise makes you smile or even laugh, that itself is a benefit. To find humour where we could find little or none before is a significant step forward.

We may have to dig through some oddities to find hidden gems and then polish them up a little to see if they are worth anything to us. This means that all the responses to the questions need to be written down. The wilder and more fanciful the responses we can find the better.

Try this:

PART 1: Allow an unhappy experience, or situation to come into your mind. Ask yourself, "What if I chose it?" "Would there be any good reason to choose it?" "Would anyone ever have a good reason to choose this?" Try not to be harsh or blaming to yourself, just be open to the possibilities.

PART 2: Ask yourself what the craziest, most far out, most "new age" person you know would say about why you chose it and write their likely responses. What would your best friend say about why you chose it? What would your favourite comedian say about why you chose it? What would a wise old man who has lived in a cave for 20 years say about why you chose it? What would a really annoying smart ass, know-it-all say about why you chose it?

Forgive God;
Forgive Yourself

*To connect with God, connect with
what is good in you.*

Forgiving God and forgiving yourself are the same thing. Here is why. Unless you can experience your own goodness you will not be able to experience the goodness of God. The extent to which you experience your own goodness is the extent to which you have awakened the facility within you to experience God's goodness. God will seem distant and remote till you have done this. Without this you will always feel like something is missing. That is true. Something is missing. Something very big is missing. God is missing and God is a lot to be missing!

Your connection with your own goodness makes God present and accessible. Accepting your own goodness and accepting God are the same thing, because God shows up inside you through your experience of your own goodness.

Forgiving yourself re-establishes your connection with your own goodness and therefore helps you reconnect with God. Letting go of the things you judge, blame and criticize yourself about allows you to reconnect with the good inside you. Forgiving God for the things you don't like about life, which you believe God created, also reconnects you to your own goodness and makes you more amenable to accepting the presence of God in your life.

We may have many ideas of how the world could be a better place. Fair enough. Yet, that may lead us to assume that God is to blame for how the world is. Perhaps the world is our way of experiencing a state other than heaven. Is the world heaven? No, obviously far from it. Therefore it is a very good chance to experience a state that is not heaven. How else could we experience a not-heaven state, except by being in one? Welcome to the not-heaven state! Are you ready to go home yet? The doorway to that home is through your connection to goodness within yourself.

If you reinforce your sense of being separate from your own goodness then you automatically separate yourself from God. If you deny your own goodness you deny God. How can it be any other way? It is simple logic. If God is good, the ultimate goodness, and you deny what is good about you then you are denying your God connection. Of course there are degrees to denying or accepting our own goodness.

We might accept our goodness in some ways, but deny it in others. We might think, "Oh I am normally quite good-natured, but I am grumpy in the early morning." Or, we might tell ourselves, "I am fine once I have had my morning coffee." We might tell ourselves that we are a failure at this or that. "I am not good with people," "I am no good with computers," and so on. However, Goodness is really about our being rather than what we do.

If we reject, or disown, the idea there is good within us, we maintain a state of feeling unworthy. Accepting our goodness also means accepting that we are worthy. This gives God somewhere to land inside us. If we believe we are unworthy because we do not match some abstract idea of "perfect", then we miss the point. We do not need to be perfect, we just need to accept the good we have inside us.

The Fame or Shame Game

Our thinking may go this way, "The world will fall at my feet, when they see how amazingly well I can sing/play guitar/play piano etc." This is an attempt to escape from shame into fame. This is not really a belief in our goodness as it depends on us doing something to earn it. We do not need to earn our goodness; we just need to learn to acknowledge it and express it. We just need to give our attention to how pleasant it is to think good thoughts, feel genuinely good feelings and do good actions. Once we get our blocks out of the way, goodness is as natural to us as breathing. We then let go of the false sense of shame and can begin to live in peace with ourselves. We also then let go of that lingering notion, which lies behind the sense of shame, that maybe we are not much good as otherwise God would not have abandoned us.

We can be blocking access to our goodness by busily pointing out to ourselves the mistakes we have made along the way. "I can't be all that good, look at the stupid thing I did." Any time we look at the idea of our own goodness unhappy memories and thoughts may come up; "I should never have said that...," "How could I be such a fool to have....," "That was bad of me to...," and so on. Forgiving ourselves includes letting go of the ways in which we habitually deny what is good about us.

What would you say to someone who constantly reminded you of all your mistakes? You would eventually tell them to shut up! You would tell them to stop it and get a life. Yet many of us put up with a voice inside us constantly reminding us of our failures – allegedly, so we won't make the same mistake again.

If you make a move to accept your goodness you may find a parade of your real or imagined failures will start marching through your mind. You may try to hide yourself from that failure parade by compulsive or addictive behaviour – which leads to more things to feel miserable about. If this happens there is no need to fight it. Just let it be part of the process of forgiving yourself, letting go and moving on.

Changing Images of Authority

A large part of the art of forgiveness is becoming reconciled with God, or with our image of God, and what we think God is. Egos are instinctively wary and fearful of anything bigger or more powerful than they are. An ego will tend to see God as simply a larger version of itself – a scary thought considering what egos can be like! To have any sense of how God actually is we need to be able to see outside of the world of the ego. The world of the ego is an experience of separation. It is a world of "me", "mine" and of "not me", "not mine". It is a phase we all go through as we develop from infants into adults. We collectively go through these infant and adult stages as a species. The current stage of our evolution shows up in the kind of world we help to create.

Egos like authority and like to be certain. Yet there is little of certainty in the world. "The only certainty is change," but that could change! It is in how we handle change and sudden unexpected events that our true morality shows.

As many were, I was very moved and inspired by the quiet dignity and decency shown by the ordinary people of Japan in handling their triple crises of earthquake, tsunami and nuclear problems. Some of my American friends said that they wished their follow countrymen could have mustered as much dignity and decency when Hurricane Katrina hit. What does it mean when people in a non-Christian country like Japan, behaves in a more "Christian" way than people in a Christian country like America? It means we get a wonderful chance to re-evaluate any lingering prejudices against other peoples and other races. We get to see that "they are not so different after all." We get delightful glimmerings of belonging to a global community.

Why does God Allow Bad Things?

"Why does God allow so much suffering in this world?", is a good question, but is also an egotistical question, because it affirms a sense of separation between God and us. The question is not usually asked in a tone of wonder or mystery. It is usually asked in a tone of complaint. That is a clue to the state of mind of the questioner. It sounds like they have come up with an answer and it is not a happy one – yet they usually do not say what their answer is.

It is fairly obvious that a large part of the suffering in the world, apart from natural disasters, is created by us humans. If everyone who asked that question changed it to, "Why do *I* allow so much suffering in this world?" and then actually did something about it, the world would be a much better place.

Much of the suffering we create as a species comes out of us being at a fairly immature stage of our evolution. If we live with a sense that we are separate from God then what will make us truly happy other than reconnecting with God? If some of the things which we chase after in order to be "happy" are actually increasing our sense of separation then it is better that we do not have those things. Some of the painful things that happen to us, turn out for the best, in hindsight.

How many times have you really wanted something and then realized later that it was far better that you did not get it? A little bit of trust in the goodness of life means we can have that kind of hindsight beforehand as foresight, as we will be more open to the good which might come out of us not getting something we want.

If you see a young child making a grab for a sharp knife and you stop it, the child will probably cry. The child does not understand that it wants something that will hurt it. We let the child go through that small suffering of not having what it wants to prevent it having more suffering of chopping bits out of itself with the knife. Sometimes life intervenes and prevents us from having things we are not ready for. It is automatic for an ego to assume that life is against it, because the ego is automatically against just about everything.

The personal suffering we most blame God for is likely either to be self-created (when we did not listen to the quiet voice inside us saying "that is not a good idea") or could well be something preventing us doing ourselves serious damage.

• • • • •

Have you ever felt like blaming God for all the bad things, which are going on around us? Take death for instance. Why have a world with a nasty thing like death? Can't we all just live forever, or something? Yes, let's do away with death. What would the world look like then? Well, it might create a few problems. It is estimated that there have been over 100 billion people born in the world since it began. That is about 14 times the current population. The world would be a bit on the full side if all those people were all still around! If many of them were making babies it would soon be a nightmare. How would we feed them all? If they could not die what would happen to them when the food runs out? Nobody would be able to move for so many people and from being weak with hunger. Sorry, but eventually we would have to re-invent death.

Disease is pretty nasty too. Let's get rid of that. What would people die from if we did not have disease? In the previous paragraph, we just re-invented death so we have to have something for people to die from. If there were lots of accidents that could take care of it, but that would be chaos. There would have to be crashes and disasters all over the place. I suppose people could just choose to die when they were ready, but that sounds a bit like suicide. Besides if earth were as crowded as it would become without disease a suicidal choice to exit might become a bit too popular. Looks like we have to re-invent disease too.

What about pain? Surely we can get rid of pain? Well, not really because we need something to tell us not to stick our hands in the fire when we want to warm them up. We also need emotional pain to let us know to stop doing something really bad for us. Looks like we are stuck with pain as well.

Of course, this is a rather flippant way to address issues that are really deep, yet, getting too heavily serious about them does not seem to help much either. If you find yourself in the middle of a dark, and murky swamp it is better to give your attention to finding the way out rather than wondering why swamps exist (and plaintively asking, "Why am I here?").

Once you are out of the swamp you can get to some high ground and get a wider perspective where things make more sense. Likewise rather than blaming God about why things like death, disasters and disease exist, it is better to align with what is good in the world, and what is good within ourselves, and let things out of our control take care of themselves till we get a better perspective.

Do You Punish Yourself?

Why would you ever want to punish yourself? What would be the point? It is like saying to yourself, "I will show you what will happen if you ever do that again!" You know not to do it again as you feel so bad about it you want to punish yourself, so punishing yourself is absurd.

You: "Don't ever do that again. Smack!"
You: "Ouch!"
You: "You better be good from now on! Smack!"
You: "Ouch! Okay, okay, please stop hitting me. I'll never do it again I promise!"

You: "Yes, you better not or you know what will happen to you!"
You: "Okay. I'll be good. Sniff…"

Maybe your idea is to get in first with a few hits to yourself as you think that God will punish you less later. Maybe you think that if you beat yourself up enough God will let you off. Did God ask you to do that? I think not. I think God would be more interested in you making amends as best you can for any harm you have done and then doing your best to move forward and create a good life. Self-bashing is just self-loathing disguised as remorse. It comes from too much self-absorption and self-indulgence. The answer is to get a life – one that is less about self and more about others.

Remorse

If you have not forgiven yourself for something the chances are that you are subtly, or overtly, punishing yourself for it. You may be using passive punishment by not letting yourself have something you want (possibly in the guise of believing you do not deserve it) or you may be punishing yourself through waves of overly dramatic remorse every time you try to move forward with your life.

Remorse is useful if it leads us to do something good in order to make amends; otherwise it is just negative self-indulgence. Remorse can be a wonderful help in getting us back on track. It can open us to having more empathy for others and being less judgmental of them when they make mistakes. Remorse can show us the way to make amends and to avoid making the same mistakes again. However, when it is not fully genuine it can be self-indulgence or arrogance in disguise. Some are so desperate to "be different" to feel that they are somehow "special" that they will even cling to a feeling of being especially bad.

It is like they want to make a big drama out of their mistakes to "prove" how bad they are as some attempt to get attention. Such wallowing can also be an excuse to avoid dealing with the realities of life. They are saying, "Look how bad and useless I am." This is not genuine remorse, which always leads out of self-absorption to more awareness of others. Remorse is also not genuine if it is more about the fear of being punished rather than real feelings of caring about those we have harmed.

Genuine remorse leads us to take action to make amends in the best way that we can given the current circumstances. If it is not possible for us to make amends directly to the one we have harmed, then we can look for an equivalent way to do so. We can do something for someone of similar age or type of person to the one we harmed and do this as a symbolic act of making amends. We can make anonymous donations to charity of an amount that makes a difference to us.

If it is impossible to make amends completely, because our behaviour was so extreme (and it is not just self created drama causing us to see it that way) then all we can do is do the best we can to lead a decent life from now on. To paraphrase the saying about vengeance, "The best remorse is a life well lived."

God's Forgiveness

In forgiving yourself you might rightly ask, "Don't I need God's forgiveness too?" Your answer to that will depend on your beliefs. It will depend on whether you see God as vengeful or compassionate. A possible answer becomes easier if we make the question clearer. How would rightness and goodness be best served? If you have made a mistake and done your best to make amends, to whomever you have wronged, then there is not much else you can do except live the best life you can.

Wallowing in guilt and shame does not do any good for anyone. It would just be more of the same self-centredness, which is usually what got us into trouble in the first place. After making amends, it is better to have faith in God's goodness and fairness and then focus our life energies on the good we can do rather than the wrong we have done.

If you feel really troubled by guilt then think through a strategy for how you can make amends. Find someone to talk it over with, or write it out (even if you decide not to show it to anyone) so you can begin to clear your way for being able to move forward. Doing the good that is within your reach is far better than bewailing harmful effects that are now out of your reach.

Spiritual Gymnasium

Imagine that this world is the spiritual equivalent of a gymnasium. We are here to develop our spiritual muscles. How do we develop a muscle? – by overcoming resistance. By overcoming things, which resist our goodness, we grow stronger in that goodness. By living in an environment, which challenges us to our core, we grow at our core. If the world were too easy it would not be doing its job. If we had never been challenged we would not have had the experience of overcoming challenges. There is an old saying, "The devil does not know who he is really working for." All the bad and negativity in the world acts as resistance and enables us to grow by pushing against it.

Developing our spiritual muscles means developing spiritual qualities. Life in the world challenges us to develop those qualities. We get challenged in our ability to be honest, kind or thoughtful in the face of temptations to be otherwise. We get challenged in being bold, courageous or confident when tempted to hide under the bedclothes instead of facing life. We get challenged to be positive and life-affirming when events only seem to show us negativity and hopelessness. In this way everything in life and every situation, even if it seems baffling, boring or bizarre, serves our evolution.

Situations that develop our spiritual muscles:

- We feel desperate for something (money, sex, fame); but only choose good and life-enhancing ways to pursue it.
- Someone tries to bully or manipulate us; we choose to stand up for ourselves.
- We see an easy way out of a difficult situation by telling a blatant lie; but we tell the truth anyway.
- We are being pressured to give up doing something we truly believe in; but we stick to our principles and keep going.
- Someone hurts us and we are tempted by vengeance; but we forgive instead.
- We overcome shyness, lack of self-esteem, or hopelessness to take action in the world in ways aligned with our highest values.
- We feel dismayed by the state of the world; yet we learn how to have fun.
- We feel really nervous about asking for a pay rise; but do it anyway.
- We see lots of evidence for how "bad" we are; but we choose to believe in our own goodness.

Just as on an individual basis we face challenges to develop spiritual qualities, likewise families, groups of people, races, nations and the whole of humanity face certain challenges as a group. Themes arise in families, sometimes going underground for a generation and then pop back up again in another generation. I was just reading a biography, *John Lennon, The Life* by Philip Norman, which illustrates this.

It starts rather simplistically by describing John Lennon as a musically gifted man from Liverpool who went to America, and toured with his band and wowed them along the way. The bizarre thing is that this was not the John Lennon we know, it was John Lennon's grandfather.

Also bizarre, is that Yoko Ono's grandfather suffered a similar fate to John Lennon's as he was also murdered by someone who was an admirer of the work for which he was well known. The book has many recurring themes throughout the generations of that family and of the people connected to it. I suspect that the lives of many of us would show recurring themes if given the same level of scrutiny as the life of John Lennon.

When we awaken to the themes and patterns within our own family, and the "groups" we belong to we begin to see patterns and are more able to find meaning behind events.

There may come a time when we can collectively learn and grow in graceful and delightful ways, rather than through suffering and difficulty. The more we are able to support each other in learning in happy ways, rather than through blame and punishment, the more we will create a world where this becomes normal. Until then, it is good to keep in mind that everything we overcome comes over to us. It becomes part of us and strengthens our spiritual development.

Reconnection with God

When we are happy we do not tend to wonder overly much about the purpose of life. Usually we wonder about the purpose of life when we feel low. Unfortunately that is the worse state in which to find, or create, any such purpose as negative attitudes will filter out the more pleasant possibilities till only the most unpleasant options are left.

At such times it is all too easy to assume that life is all misery, drudgery and pointlessness – and that is on a good day! If that is going on it is tempting to see life as a bad joke and to resent God for putting us here. This is like sticking our head down the toilet and then blaming God for how bad life looks.

It is good to remember that just because we don't see our life purpose does not mean that it is not present. The earlier analogy of life as a spiritual gymnasium helps shine some light on this issue too. If the purpose of life is to develop a range of spiritual qualities, then life is perfectly set up to help us do that. No matter how tedious, banal, or meaningless life may seem in our worst moments we can still be growing tremendously.

Even in those moments of our worst days of grumpiness, anger or irritation we can be making immense strides without realizing it. If, that is, we make an effort to make something out of the situation and not just play victim. If we choose to think and act in a creative way we are acting as "creators".

Another name for God is "The Creator". That is a very big hint about one aspect to the purpose of life: to learn to create. When we get to the point of, "I am fed up complaining about this. I am going to do something about it." When we decide, "Life feels so pointless just now, but I think I will go and plant a tree," "Look how irritable I am getting, I think I will give myself a treat to cheer myself up."

When we make those kinds of changes within ourselves we are learning to move and shift energy in a very direct way. We are learning to be creators and shapers of energy. We are also learning to convert our personal reactions into spiritual qualities. Qualities like compassion, good humour, patience, tolerance, spontaneity, boldness, courage and the like emerge as the gifts we gain from the situation we are in.

The very circumstances that test us to our limits are what helps us to increase our limits. We find afterwards that we are bigger and can handle more. What we thought was too much is now something we can cope with as we have developed the qualities to handle it. When standing in a queue we can cultivate patience or we can just remain irritated. It is our choice.

There is a way out even if you are in circumstances where you really feel completely stuck and helpless, or in a situation you find disturbing or challenging. Discover and learn to express the spiritual qualities that experience is meant to teach you, and you will exit that situation like a cork out of a champagne bottle. Where there seems to be no way out, suddenly the way will appear. Where everything seemed impossible; everything will seem possible. Having found your ability to get to the cause behind events, you will be much more amenable to truly connecting with the larger life we call God.

Do you really want to reconnect with God? It is possible that you might feel ambivalent about it. "What if I don't like it, can I go back to where I was?" What can get in the way are the old concepts of God that we have inherited, where God is presented like some ghastly mediaeval King with a liking for brutality and torture. Yes, we better love Him, and quickly, or who knows what he is going to do to us! "Oh no, He can read my thoughts! I'm really in for it now!" You may have a wall of resentment, which stops you approaching God.

That resentment comes from painful experiences in life that make no sense to you. It may come from people who have hurt you "in God's name." You may have become frightened of God because your experience of others having power over you was not pleasant. It is not God's fault that some of those who claim to be his representatives on earth are stupid, devious, or just plain evil.

Such people like to present God as an exaggerated version of themselves to justify their behaviour. Many of them are focused on power rather than love and so do not make good representatives of God as they don't have a clue about unconditional love.

When looking at our relationship with God we can find ourselves in a dilemma: "I want to be totally one with everything; and I want to be totally separate from everything." We want to connect with our source, but we don't want to lose who we are in the process. Yet, the process of reconnection is not as threatening as it might seem. From one angle reconnection with God is not necessary as we are always connected.

As we get better at hearing the quiet voice within us, which guides us to the light, we realize that it has always been there. Sometimes the demands of the world get in the way. Sometimes even the voice of our social conscience can get in the way. Yet, when we begin to listen to what our inner sense of rightness, which some call The God Within, is telling us, we become more at-one with God. We realize that what is best for us harmonizes with what is best for all.

It is really so simple; listen to the Goodness within you, trust and take action. "What if I make a mistake?" you might ask. The biggest mistake you can make in your life is to not make enough mistakes, because that means you are living too fearfully (of course some live life too recklessly, but if you are the cautious type that is not you). You learn nothing from the mistakes you do not make. Naturally, we can still use religious books and teachings to uphold us through times when we are not clear, or when life gets confusing and particularly challenging. Yet, more and more we find that what guides us is an inner knowing. That inner knowing is our connection with Goodness, which is our connection with God.

The connection with God that is most immediately available, when we awaken to it and live in harmony with it, is our own sense of Goodness. We also realize that Goodness is the Goodness in everyone and is not exclusive to us. Some people are more awake to it than others, but the Goodness is always there – somewhere.

Reconnecting with God is easier if you put aside thinking of God as some form of strict parent ready to leap on every mistake you make – and ready to judge you for every mistake you ever made. It does not make sense for God to create creatures who are very fallible, and vulnerable to error, and then punish them for the very mistakes which they must inevitably make.

God's message to humanity is not about judgment and punishment as some would have us believe. God's message to you is much kinder than that. It can be expressed as a restatement of a saying from long ago. *"You are my beloved child in whom I am well pleased."*

Try this:

1. Can you put aside any false modesty and feel a sense of Goodness inside you? If so how can you cultivate it and let it grow in you?

2. Can you see ways that the challenges in your life contribute to your spiritual development and how the challenges in the world contribute to humanity's spiritual development?

Forgiveness as
an Act of Power

When we forgive we choose to be empowered,
rather than being a victim.

In exploring forgiveness we come to see that our general attitude plays a large part in how easily we can forgive. Forgiveness is always possible, yet there are attitudes and inner abilities which we can cultivate which makes forgiveness easier. By developing those attitudes, by becoming more accepting, less judgemental, less cynical, and becoming kinder to ourselves, we make forgiveness more accessible and achievable rather than elusive and mysterious.

You might wonder, "Why focus so much on forgiveness rather than love? Would not a focus on love be just as effective?" Such a focus can certainly help. However, improving our capacity to forgive helps us get to a place inside of us where we can love more deeply, openly and widely. Forgiveness is an aspect of our capacity to love. Learning to forgive makes us more able to love. It helps us take our capacity to love from the romantic level to the spiritual level. The more we are able to move away from fear, hatred, and resentment the more we move towards love.

The more we can forgive the more we love without it being tainted by a personal agenda. The more we can forgive we can love the people we already know and the more we can love different types of people.

Focusing on forgiveness gives us practical and immediate steps to improve our current relationships – which after all is an expression of love, even if of an impersonal kind, in the nitty-gritty of daily life. It helps us transform situations and relationships and frees up the inner resources we need to have a happier and healthier life. Besides there are people we may be ready to forgive who we are not ready to love – at least at this time. Since forgiveness helps us create better relationships this naturally means we can be more loving.

We have also been exploring how becoming reconciled with ourselves not only makes it easier to be able to forgive ourselves, but also makes it easier to forgive others. Having a friendly relationship with the various qualities and quirks which go to make up our human nature creates a good foundation for a forgiving attitude. When we are divided within ourselves it is harder to find the inner capacity to forgive. Becoming reconciled with ourselves and increasing our capacity to forgive go hand in hand.

Early on we explored some of the benefits to forgiving. As we practise forgiveness we become less prone to fear and guilt. We become immune to attempts to manipulate us as fear and guilt are the usual weapons of choice of manipulators. As we become more happy and at peace with ourselves we also become more willing to support others in being happy and at peace too. Forgiveness enables us to take back the power in our lives. Those who seemed to have a lot of power over us, suddenly have no real power when we can truly forgive and lose our fear of them.

Is it good to look at forgiveness as an act of power? Perhaps we think that we should only forgive out of high-minded ideals, or that we should only forgive for the benefit of others. Yet this has not brought us the results we want. Many of us are not as forgiving as we would like to be. If we look at our own life, and what goes on in our mind, we can see that high-minded ideals have not been enough.

We often told ourselves that we "should" forgive someone, yet found ourselves struggling, or totally unable to do so. Forgiveness can set us free, and now we know how to do it we can free ourselves from getting trapped in pain, guilt and shame. Forgiveness is an attitude of mind as much as a specific action we can take. Specific acts of forgiveness help us cultivate a forgiving attitude. By deciding to adopt a forgiving attitude to an experience, and resolving and releasing our unforgiving thoughts and feelings around it, we become more able to hold this attitude - or rather hold this *altitude*.

We are building our forgiveness capability every time we forgive. Every time we forgive it not only becomes easier to forgive again, it becomes easier to hold a forgiving attitude. In this way forgiveness becomes a proactive and dynamic way of living.

We may wonder whether we will be taken advantage of if we become more forgiving. We may feel that we have to maintain a tough stance so that our good nature will not be abused. If we look more closely we may well find that it is our capacity for foolishness that gets us into trouble rather than our capacity for forgiveness. A genuinely forgiving attitude brings a capacity to understand and empathize with others. This enables us to have much more insight into other people's thoughts, feelings and behaviour.

We become much more aware of how others are likely to behave and can make wiser decisions. We are more able to see whether someone is genuinely honest and trustworthy. With a forgiving attitude, we are more likely to see beyond someone's outward personality to see whether they have the necessary qualities in their character to do what they say they will do. We can make choices based on our insight. We may decide not to create a personal, social or business relationship based on what we see, or we may discuss any potential problems we anticipate with them, or we can decide to give them the benefit of the doubt and go ahead anyway.

As we become more forgiving and more reconciled with ourselves we become less dependent on others for approval. We then become more able to live our own highest ideals and aspirations without constantly looking around to check what others will think. We can begin to live the life we were meant to live and engage our full creative capacity whether that is in small things or in large things.

Learning to forgive is work. Yet it is work of the noblest and most beneficial kind. Forgiveness allows us to access the best within us and to access the best in others. It frees us from the past and enables us to be present in the moment. This is what forgiveness enables us to do, and anything that does this can be considered a power.

Therefore, Forgiveness is Power. It is the Power to lift ourselves out of the maze created by the types of thinking which are conditioned by the present cultural norms. Forgiveness is the power to decide how our experiences shape our character and our perspective on life. It is the power to live life as we were meant to live it: in freedom, peace and happiness. Forgiveness is the power to live and to love fully and completely.

As you deepen your experience of forgiveness, through exploring the ideas and exercises you have come across in this book, you will be well on your way to becoming as forgiving as you would like to be. By letting forgiveness be a topic of conversation in your life (online or off-line) you will connect with others in deeper and richer ways. By doing so you are affirming that forgiveness is practical, usable and accessible.

This alone can help to create change.

Sometimes simply saying to people that you are reading a book about forgiveness will trigger something healing within them. As you share your forgiveness experiences, and your own insights, it will change your life for the better and help change the world for the better.

Are you really as forgiving as you would like to be?

The choice is now yours.

Forgiveness Toolkit

Forgiveness Toolkit

Scattered through the various chapters you will find examples of techniques and methods to enhance your capacity to forgive. Here are some more to try; see what appeals to you. Play with them, adjust them to fit your needs and see what new insights and new sense of freedom comes to you.

Heavenly Perspective

Situations can look very different when we look at them with a detached perspective. When we detach from a situation, without denying that it happened, we can then begin to let go of our reactions and be at peace with it. We all benefit from seeing the bigger picture. We will see the events on earth very differently when we view them from the perspective of heaven. Yet, we do not have to wait to gain the benefits of having that heavenly perspective – we can have it now.

Try this:

1. Imagine you are up in heaven sitting in a Viewing Room. You are watching something on a screen. What you are watching is an event you need to forgive. Sitting behind you is an angel spreading wings of peaceful, healing energy over you, and sitting beside you (but not too close) is the person you need to forgive. Imagine the person seeing what they did from your point of view and feeling everything that you felt. Imagine the look of regret and consternation on their face about what they did.

After seeing the whole thing from start to finish the person now turns to you. What do they say?

2. Now imagine that the angel shows you what was going on in that person's life up to that point. You are shown what they were thinking and feeling and what they believe caused them to behave that way. Do you have anything to say to them?

Resizing

It is harder to forgive something if it looms large in our mind. Bullies may seem huge and dominating. Bad experiences can seem very dark and forbidding. We size an event by how large, dark or heavy we portray it in our mind. The large size in which we often cast painful events in our minds makes it harder to face them and harder to forgive them.

In essence we are showing ourselves how we feel about the event, and about the participants, by how we portray the various characters in our minds. How we represent things inwardly is a gateway to how we feel about them. We can use this to our advantage because if we change how we portray something internally this will change how we feel about the situation altogether. Making something smaller and lighter in the way we look at it makes it have less impact on us. This method is very similar to some of the methods used in systems like NLP (Neuro-Linguistic Programming).

Try this:

- Close your eyes and imagine an event you need to forgive.
- Notice how you represent the event in your mind. Notice the bigness of it. Notice the darkness and heaviness of it. Now shrink everything down till it gets smaller and smaller. If there are people involved imagine them as very tiny and saying whatever they said in a tiny squeaky voice. If this makes you laugh, all the better.
- Take a few deep breaths, rest a moment, and run through the event again. Notice how big they appear in your imagination and shrink them again, tiny voice and all. Try this a few times.
- Now think of the event again. How do you feel this time? With a bit of practice much, or all, of the sting will come out of it. You could then apply one of the forgiveness techniques, covered in other chapters, to the event to dissolve the impact further.

Forgiving Groups

Sometimes we need to forgive groups or whole races of people. We may need to forgive a group of people who at different times acted out a common theme. Such groups could be: "All those people who never appreciated or valued me." Or, "All those people who never encouraged me to be my best." "All those people who did not support me, but who could have," and so on. The group can also be "men", "women", "rich people", "beggars", "homeless people" and so on.

We may need to forgive people of a particular race or religion, or from a particular country. We may notice that we have a tendency to look down on people from another race or religion, or another area and think scornfully of them.

This type of pattern of unforgiveness tends to be ongoing and since there are a number of potential targets this makes it easy for us to gather information to support our judgements and ignore any other information. When our unforgiving mind is active we tend to minimize the importance of, or filter out completely, those things we see which contradict our unforgiving attitudes and amplify or exaggerate the importance of those things we notice which confirm it.

Try this:

Is there a group of people, race or creed that you need to forgive?

1. Can you think of something you saw or heard which contradicts your predominant ideas about those people? Do you genuinely believe that those people are all bad, are always bad and never do anything good? Is how they related to *you* the only thing that is important about those people? If you had been different, could they have been different?

2. Think of this group and notice the effect it has on your body. Take some deep breaths and breathe out the sensations. As you breathe out start to let go of the feelings by affirming (out loud or silently), "I forgive this situation and release these feelings." You could also try telling yourself, "You forgive this situation and release these feelings, " and see what works best for you.

Fireworks

This exercise helps you clear and release pain, feeling stuck, or any sense of discomfort that you are experiencing in your body. It is very satisfying and a lot of fun too. It is a little bit involved so read through a few times before trying it, or go through it slowly step-by-step, to get the idea.

Sit somewhere away from distractions and take your time. Allow each step to take at least one breath cycle (one breath in and one breath out). Use your imagination to see or feel each of the steps.

1. Notice a place in your body where you feel some kind of discomfort. It might be an ache, a pain, or whatever. If there is more than one choose the one that is most uncomfortable.
2. Imagine yourself wrapping white bandages around the discomfort. Even

if the discomfort is deep inside your body just imagine the bandages going closely around it anyway.

3. Imagine that the bandages start to shrink, meld together, and tighten around the discomfort. They take on the shape of it and contain it like it is a package wrapped in bandages.

4. Imagine that you are now lifting that package out of your body and placing it about ten metres in front of you. Please note that you are only imagining lifting the uncomfortable feeling in that part of your body, not imagining lifting that part of your body itself.

5. Imagine the package shooting straight up high into the air where it goes through a horizontal barrier into an area of translucent purple light. The package suddenly starts to go off like a firework display and disintegrates while making many very satisfying flashes, fizzes, bangs, cracks and pops. Allow a few breaths for this.

6. You see any waste from the explosions fall back to the earth, as ash, well away from you. This is other people's energy and no longer concerns you. You also see sparkles of bright golden light coming down. This is your own energy transformed. As you breathe in you easily pull the golden sparkles of light towards you. You let these sparkles flow back into where you originally felt discomfort and let them heal and regenerate that area.

You may need to do this exercise a number of times for it to have an effect, but sometimes you will feel the difference right away. As you get used to doing it you may not need to do the exercise sitting down. With practise it is even possible to do this exercise while walking.

Sitting Comfortably

There is a natural goodness that is available to us at any time. We may miss even noticing it if we get too busy with struggling and striving.

This kind of goodness is simple and subtle. It takes virtually no effort to contact it. Mostly we just need to become aware of it and use our awareness to let it expand. The more we are aware of it the more it grows.

Any challenge we might have in this process will come from it being so easy. We can become used to assuming that there has to be some kind of effort in order to get to feeling good. We may wonder, "Am I doing it right? Is it really this easy?" We may get distracted by lots of thoughts, or feeling that we ought to be "doing something." If that happens don't fight it. Just notice it and come back to how nice it is to feel comfortable.

What makes this a deeply spiritual process is that we are letting go of being driven and making space within ourselves for renewal of our connection with our own life force. This process helps us step out of the roles and patterns of thinking and feeling that we normally inhabit and have a fresh experience. We are then more able to accept life as it is and more able to forgive.

Try this:

Give yourself 5 minutes or 10 minutes of uninterrupted space.

1. Sit comfortably and notice how good it feels to do just that. Notice how good it is just to feel comfortable. If you find yourself wanting to sigh or yawn let that happen.

2. Scan your body from head to toe and notice the places where you feel the most comfortable. As you breathe gently pause on the out breath and rest your awareness on where you feel most comfortable in your body. If the feeling of "most comfortable" moves then move your attention with it.

Finding Natural
Goodness

Among all the tendencies we find within ourselves there is a tendency to goodness. Even if this gets covered up with layers of negativity of various kinds, it is still there. This tendency to goodness burns within us just waiting for us to give it attention so that it can grow.

It can be all too easy for awareness of our personal problems and seeming inadequacies to dominate our thinking about ourselves. We can get entangled in a perpetual round of "fixing" ourselves when really what we most need to do is acknowledge our goodness and allow it to flow and grow.

Even those of us who believe things like, "You get more of what you focus on," and "Energy follows thought," can still end up focusing on what we see as being "not right" about ourselves rather than on what is right about ourselves. Likewise we can get so caught up with the problems in the world that we lose sight of the beauty and magnificence of life that is all around us.

Here are some exercises to help us reconnect with the goodness within ourselves and the goodness in life.

Goodness Inside

What is good, kind, and helpful inside you? What awakens you to beauty and wonder? Who or what most easily bring up those feelings? Put your attention on what brings up those feelings the most easily at this moment.

Notice in your body where these feelings arise (often it is the chest or in the belly). Is there an image that you can easily associate with that feeling? For a few minutes just hold that feeling or that image and breathe into it.

Goodness Outside

If possible do this outside in a garden, park or nature spot. Find something natural which appeals to you. It can be looking at a plant, a tree, or watching a bird or wild animal. It can be a river, a stream flowing or watching the ocean waves. It can be watching the clouds go by, or looking at a sunset or sunrise. It can be looking at reeds or ducks swimming in a pond, or the ripples on the surface caused by the wind.

Notice that there is something intrinsically good about it. It is like there is a goodness underlying what is going on. Just notice that feeling, that sense of goodness. It might be very slight and only for a fraction of a second at first, but play with it and it will grow.

Connecting with God

What if God were already present in your life? What if God were already present in your body?

If God were even already present in your body, would you be able to sense it? Would connecting with God feel pleasant or unpleasant? Let's assume it would be pleasant and explore that possibility.

Give yourself 5 or 10 minutes to do this.

- Take a few deep breaths, letting go with a sigh each time.
- Just sit and notice a feeling of Pleasantness inside your body. It could be in your hands, your feet, your chest or your belly. Just gently look for a subtle sense of Pleasantness and rest your attention on it.
- Various thoughts and feelings will come up as you are doing this. Just notice which is more pleasant, the thought or feeling which has arisen or the Pleasantness, and choose the one you want.

What can help with this exercise is to put your attention into both your hands and your feet at the same time that you are doing it. This takes a little bit of practice but it helps diffuse your awareness so that you don't get too heavily focused.

You may find that this practice eventually leads to being aware of Something Within you which is beyond words, but which is very pleasant to contact. The pleasant feeling may be very subtle at first but will slowly grow as you give it attention. You may even find that this process works even if the actual source of the pleasant feeling turns out to be something mundane (such as warmth from a nearby heater) as it is your intention that makes it work.

A Reconciled Life

One of the underlying themes of this book is that the more we are reconciled and at peace with life, and the process of living, the more forgiving we can be. The more we find meaning in events, the more we find fulfilment as we proceed along our life path. The more we feel fulfilled the more we want to extend fulfilment to others and the more forgiving we become.

One way to experience meaning, as outlined in the *Be Wounded, or Be Wise* chapter, is to look at what spiritual quality an event calls for us to express. In this way we begin to co-operate with the underlying purpose in our life. However, we can take this a step further. Rather than wait for a specific event to come along and trigger the development of a particular quality we can actively look to what quality would most enhance our life at this time and specifically look for ways to awaken it.

A useful analogy is that there are two ways which fire can be created via simple objects. It can be created through rubbing two sticks together, "Fire by Friction", or by using a piece of glass to focus the light of the sun, "Solar Fire". Likewise our inner fire, our consciousness, can either we awakened via Fire by Friction or by Solar Fire. Fire by Friction is when we reach an awakening or realization via "rubbing" against other people and the events of life; Solar Fire is when we deliberately participate in the awakening of our consciousness by focusing the light within us through the "lens" of our mind.

When we deliberately decide to develop a particular spiritual quality, and give attention to that process, we are then using Solar Fire, which is a much more effective and more comfortable way to grow in awareness than Fire by Friction.

Many people have already awakened to using this principle of Solar Fire without giving it that name or even any name. To use the principle of Solar Fire we only need to take a few simple steps. We just need to decide which spiritual quality would most enhance our life at this time and then explore ways to cultivate it. A clue can be… where in life are we experiencing the most emotional pain and suffering? If we are experiencing the most pain in our relationships we can look to what quality would liberate us from that pain. It could be we need to learn acceptance, detachment, or to be more forgiving. If we are experiencing most of our pain around lacking a sense of purpose we can look to that area to see what quality we can develop which would help.

It could be we need to learn surrender, appreciation, or self-acceptance. If we experience most of our pain through being too afraid to express our inner gifts then the qualities we need to develop could be courage, boldness and confidence.

If the answer is not obvious then we need to explore and work with it to discover the underling theme. We do not need to get it exactly right. We can work on one quality and later switch to another, or work on a few at the same time as we go along. Having discovered a likely contender we then explore ways to cultivate it. Active qualities may need to be acted out in order to develop them. Boldness and courage can be developed simply by moving boldly and courageously. That is why armies march boldly and tribes have aggressive tribal dances – especially before going to war.

Qualities can also be developed by putting our attention on them via reading stories of people who have expressed those qualities. Reading the biography of someone who embodies that quality is a good way to connect with it. In fact reading the biography of someone who successfully faced challenges in the area of life you want to work on can give you clues as to what qualities you can develop to handle it.

Finding a symbol for a quality, such as an animal, an angel ("Angel of Abundance", "Angel of Play") or whatever also helps you focus on the quality. We don't have to be heavily serious about our search as by the act of searching we are already on our way.

The use of sound can also be a way to express a quality. Recently I wanted to develop more of a sense of appreciation. I noticed that an "Mmmmm" sound seemed to me to go with that quality. (I think of it as the yummy food sound: The sound people make when enjoying good food.) I use that "Mmmm" sound to help me develop the quality of appreciation by sitting for 10 or 15 minutes each day and happily going "Mmmmm". (I stop sooner if it feels tiring.) I do it silently or outwardly depending on the situation. It gives me a feeling of warm appreciation for life.

For some a colour, shape or object could represent the quality they need. What is important is to have a way of putting our attention on the quality we want to develop. Anything which appeals to us, and which helps keep our attention on that quality, is suitable for this purpose.

Try this:

Pick a situation in your life that you would like to transform. What spiritual quality will help you? If it is not obvious be open to exploring till you get at least a rough idea. Is it an active dynamic quality or a more quiet receptive one? Ponder on how you can develop that quality. Do you need to move in order to ground it, or just find a way to contemplate it? Is there a sound, colour, image, animal or anything that could represent that quality to you and remind you of it during the day? How can you include the things that represent that quality into your life more?

How will your life be when you express that quality? How will you walk, stand, talk and behave? How will you feel as you fully embody that quality? Make up a ten minute-long exercise (either moving or sitting) you can use to ground that quality and do it every day for at least a month. Vary it if it gets boring.

Selected Bibliography

William Bloom, *Endorphin Effect*, Piatkus, 2011.

Robert Bly, *Iron John: A Book About Men*, De Capo Press, 2004.

Dr David Burns, *Feeling Good, The New Mood Therapy*, Avon Books/Harper Collins, 2008.

Erika Chopich, Margaret Paul, *Healing Your Aloneness*, Harper Collins, 1990.

Michael Deida, *The Way of the Superior Man*, Sounds True, 2004.

T Harv Eker, *Secrets of the Millionaire Mind*, Harper Collins, 2005.

Louise Hay, *You Can Heal Your Life*, Hay House, 2009.

Robert Holden, *Happiness Now*, Hay House, 2007.

Robert Kiyosaki, *Rich Dad Poor Dad*, Plata Publishing, 2011.

Caroline Myss, *Why People Don't Heal and How They Can*, Three River Press, 2009.

Anthony Robbins, *Awaken the Giant Within: How to Take Immediate Control of Your Mental, Emotional, Physical and Financial Life*, Pocket Books, 2001.

Dorothy Rowe, *Depression: The Way out of Your Prison*, Routledge & Kegan Paul, 2011.

Dr. Helen Schucman, *A Course in Miracles*, Foundation for Inner Peace, 2007.

Wallace D. Wattles, *The Science of Getting Rich*, Textbook Classics, 2013 (and various others, including free downloads).

About the Author

Community life offers continual lessons in Forgiveness. William Martin's experience of over 30 years involvement with the Findhorn community is thus encapsulated within these pages. He has had many roles within the community including working in the famous gardens, managing the computer department and at one point having the grandly titled role Chairman of the Executive Committee. He also worked within the computer field as a freelance IT specialist to BT, and Apple Computer UK. Additionally, he gave innovative courses that combined computer training with personal development where trainees gained self-esteem while they gained computer skills.

Although an enthusiastic student of *A Course in Miracles* for over three decades his experiences of traveling in Asia led him to see that an open and secular approach to Forgiveness would help many people not engaged by most of the currently available material. He created this practical user guide to help make Forgiveness usable and accessible by anyone – no matter their faith or philosophy.

William regards himself as a beginner in the art of Forgiveness who is happy to help other beginners.

He blogs and tweets about Forgiveness and all things life enhancing.

BLOG: williamfergusmartin.com,

TWITTER: WillFMartin

For more on *Forgiveness is Power* and especially on using the Four Steps to Forgiveness: forgiveness-is-power.com and hashtag #fipwm.

William is happy to write bespoke articles, give talks and do interviews.

Further Findhorn Press Titles

Ho'oponopono by Ulrich E. Duprée

Powerful yet concise, this revolutionary guide summarizes the Hawaiian ritual of forgiveness and offers methods for immediately creating positive effects in everyday life. Exploring the concept that everyone is deeply connected — despite feelings of singularity and separation — four tenets are disclosed for creating peace with oneself and others: I am sorry, Please forgive me, I love you, and Thank you.

978-1-84409-597-1

The Gift of Forgiveness by Olivier Clerc

Ten years ago, Olivier Clerc went to Teotihuacan, Mexico, to follow a week-long Toltec workshop with Don Miguel Ruiz. During that time he experienced a powerful and life-changing process: The Gift of Forgiveness. In this short but intense book, Clerc now shares with us this unique and simple Toltec tool, which can bring much relief, forgiveness and love into our lives, as it has in his own life and that of the other participants.

978-1-84409-190-4

FINDHORN PRESS

Life-Changing Books

For a complete catalogue,
please contact:

Findhorn Press Ltd
117-121 High Street,
Forres IV36 1AB,
Scotland, UK

t +44 (0)1309 690582
f +44 (0)131 777 2711
e info@findhornpress.com

or consult our catalogue online
(with secure order facility) on
www.findhornpress.com

For information on the Findhorn Foundation:
www.findhorn.org